THE PARKER PRINCIPLES

10 Leadership Force Multipliers

Lessons in Leadership: Airborne Ranger to CEO

By Mel Parker

Copyright

Cover Art By: Charala

Dedication

With all my heart and my love, this book is dedicated to my Grandmother Augusta M Robinson (August 31, 1919 to October 28, 2016).

"Precious in the sight of the Lord is the death of his Saints"
Psalm 116:15

You literally saved my life. You were my rock and my Christian foundation. You loved me relentlessly. You protected and inspired me. The power of your faith and humility forged the true core of who I am and the man I strive to be. I promised you this book, and you just *don't* break promises to Grandma. I live everyday knowing you are watching over me and trying to make you proud.

I Love You!

Recognizing that I volunteered as a Ranger, fully knowing the hazards of my chosen profession, I will always endeavor to uphold the prestige, honor and high esprit de corps of my Ranger regiment.

Acknowledging the fact that a Ranger is a more elite soldier, who arrives at the cutting edge of battle by land, sea, or air, I accept the fact that as a Ranger, my country expects me to move further, faster, and fight harder than any other soldier.

Never shall I fail my comrades. I will always keep myself mentally alert, physically strong and morally straight, and I will shoulder more than my share of the task, whatever it may be, one hundred percent and then some.

Gallantly will I show the world that I am a specially selected and well trained soldier. My courtesy to superior officers, neatness of dress, and care of equipment shall set the standard for others to follow.

Energetically will I meet the enemies of my country. I shall defeat them on the field of battle for I am better trained and will fight with all my might. Surrender is not a Ranger word. I will never leave a fallen comrade to fall into the hands of the enemy and under no circumstances will I ever embarrass my country.

Readily will I display the intestinal fortitude required to fight on to the Ranger objective and complete the mission, though I be the lone survivor.

RANGERS LEAD THE WAY

About the Author

Mel Parker is the Founder, President, and Chief Executive Officer of Take The Limits Off LLC, an organization dedicated to expanding the efficiency and effectiveness of Leaders and to the ever-evolving and transforming Art of Leadership. Mr. Parker has delivered leadership expertise through panels, seminars, and keynote addresses specially focusing on: Inspirational Leadership, High Performance Teams, Transformational Change, and Crisis Leadership. Mel has been featured in *Black Enterprise*, *Savoy*, and *Vetrepreneur* magazines. Along with various military and civilian awards, Mr. Parker was also named one of the Top 100 Most Influential Blacks in Corporate America in 2012 and then again 2014.

Mel graduated from the United States Military Academy at West Point as a Second Lieutenant in the Field Artillery and served in the elite 82nd Airborne Division. During his service, he graduated from Airborne School, Ranger School, and Airborne Operations School. Mel is a combat veteran having served in Iraq and Kuwait during Operations Desert Storm and Desert Shield.

Mel has held senior leadership positions in some of the world's best companies to include: PepsiCo, Corporate Express/Staples, Newell Rubbermaid, Dell Computers, and Brink's:

- **Pepsi**
    - General Manager
    - Gatorade Business Manager
    - Kroger Team Leader
- **Corporate Express**
    - VP & GM North America Commercial Office Products
- **Newell Rubbermaid**
    - VP Sales & Channel Marketing North America
- **Dell Consumer and Small Office**
    - VP & GM North America
- **Brinks**
    - President of North America

Mel's International experience includes managing teams in:

- South America
- India
- Philippines
- North Africa.

He has conducted executive MBA studies at CKGSB – China School of Business – Shanghai, China, SKOLKOVO – Moscow School of Management – Moscow, Russia, ISB - India School of Business – Hyderabad, India.

Mel serves on the Board of Directors for Vectrus (NYSE: VEC). Vectrus delivers global infrastructure, IT and logistics services primarily to the Department of Defense. He also serves on the Board of the National Black MBA Association and served on the Executive Advisory Board for Big Brothers/Big Sisters of Central Texas.

Table of Contents

Acknowledgments

First, I thank God, my Lord and Savior, for all that I am and all that I have achieved.

I want to thank Dee, my wife of multiple decades and the most important person in my life. My lifelong lover, friend, confidant, mentor, and protector. My sons, Jovann and Jereaud, and the joys of my life, my grandsons, Jaden and Giovanni.

I want to thank my grandmother, who singlehandedly loved me through the most trying times of my childhood as she literally changed the direction of my life. Through establishing a Christian foundation, she ingrained in me an overall belief in the dignity and "goodness" of people and showed me that humility equals strength and that love triumphs over all.

I want to thank my high school football coach, Bruce McFerren, who showed me the advantage of being a student-athlete to realize my dreams. Go Westover Wolverines!

I want to thank the late Senator Jesse A. Helms – former five term senator from North Carolina, widely known as the most racially polarizing senator to have served in this era. Yes, Senator Helms, for some reason still unknown, chose to submit me as his principal nominee to the United States Military Academy in 1984. Being his principal nominee afforded me the opportunity to compete and receive consideration for an early acceptance and appointment, which I received in December of 1984. The Senator Helms nomination caused shock, awe, and disbelief throughout my family and community. It is both honorable and principled to give credit where credit is due. Thank you, Senator Helms.

There is a whole cadre of military leaders I want to thank for their support and mentorship in shaping me as a leader. Special Note: All titles represent their rank at the time they intersected with my life.

- CPT Bill Harner, my D-4 Tactical Officer at the Academy responsible for preparing Cadet Parker to be 2nd Lt. Parker. Go Dukes!

- My leaders from the 82nd Airborne – LTC Bruce A. Brant, MAJ James L Cobb, CPT Anthony A. Layton, CPT Paul H. Slinkerd III and CPT Henry Bennett. Airborne All the Way!

Special thanks to all present and past Ranger Instructors at the US Army Ranger School. These are easily the most hardcore, honorable, and professional soldiers I have ever encountered, and they run the absolute best leadership school on the planet. These individuals ensure every military person that wears the Ranger tab... earned the Ranger tab. Rangers Lead the Way!

There is also a cadre of corporate leaders I would stack up against any leader at any company on the planet. At PepsiCo – Kevin Walling (the human resources leader that hired me for my first job in corporate America), Kurt Chebatoris, Trevor Toolson and Mike Cooke. At Corporate Express/Staples Jay Mutschler – the best boss I have ever had. At Dell Michael Dell, Steve Felice and Steve Price and at Brink's Tom Schievelbein.

There are so many people that have made significant contributions into the leader I am today; it was hard to leave anyone out... although I am sure I missed someone important... as my grandson Jaden would say... My Bad! Okay, I know this is probably starting to sound like acceptance remarks at the "Emmy's". I hear the music playing so I will exit... stage left.

Preface

What seems like many moons ago, I had just finished my first notable keynote presentation of *The Parker Principles* to over 1,000 MBAs. While I believed in the leadership value of the information I shared with these MBAs, I was still stunned to receive a standing ovation. While it was embarrassingly long, I will never forget the honor I felt, providing value and being of service. Today, even as a seasoned public speaker, these standing ovations leave me humbled.

I was shocked at what happened next. It is standard procedure to hang around after my seminars and presentations to connect personally with the audience (meet, greet and shake). Usually, there are 5 or 10 energized souls that hang around to ask questions and chat, but this time was different. I noticed a line starting to form, a very long line. There were dozens and dozens of MBAs of every age and stage in their career waiting in line to meet... me.

Wow, this was new.

During the hour or so it took to get through the line, I was asked no less than a dozen times. When am I going to write a book on *The Parker Principles*? When am I going to go deeper into the principles and their best practices? Frankly, I had never considered the idea of a book. Each time the idea was mentioned, I would do research and note there are over 100,000 books on leadership from educators, managers, and executives, so what would be my differentiated value add? What would a book from me provide that the other 100,000 do not?

I think I realized that day for the first time that the differentiated value add was me. My life experience, my journey, and my common-sense principled approach to leadership that has been tested and proven successful.

I could tell from the comments and conversation of the day that my message resonated and found its mark with the audience. That an ordinary person from very humble beginnings can be blessed with an extraordinary career grounded in faith, leadership, and humility. People saw some part of themselves in my story and felt "that if Mel can do it...then so can I"."

The concept of sharing myself and my journey could actually make a difference. This felt like purpose, a mission, or maybe even a calling. While I felt inspired to write this book, the magnitude of making this a reality seemed daunting.

It was clear the world probably didn't need another how to manual on climbing the corporate ladder or winning in the corporate world. But maybe, just maybe, sharing the learnings, mistakes, successes and failures I've experienced along my journey would have value.

So, here I am, sharing my journey.

Make no mistake. I'm not here to show you how to be a corporate ladder climbing ninja, but I do believe if you unlock the true potential of your leadership, your ascension up the ladder will be swift. This is a book about Leadership; more specifically, it is about *Taking The Limits Off* Leadership.

What is T.T.L.O. Leadership? That's a great question. The answer is a bit nuanced. While TTLO Leadership is my own creation, I would describe it as a hybrid leadership style grounded in the philosophies and principles of both *Inspirational Leadership* and *Servant Leadership*.

Inspirational Leadership, as defined by the National Research Council, is "**energizing** and creating a sense of direction for your employees and **excitement and momentum for change.**" It involves energizing individuals to **strive toward a compelling vision** of the future. It includes offering **clarity** around goals and objectives and ensuring those who are led work **collaboratively** towards a **shared purpose**. It also includes the provision of required resources and

2

motivational support that employees need to grow, along with the **empowerment** and **accountability** for them to **take responsibility** for their own success.

Servant Leadership, as defined and coined by Robert K. Greenleaf and the Center for Servant Leadership, "is a philosophy and set of practices **that enriches the lives of individuals, builds better organizations** and ultimately creates a more caring world."

TTLO Leadership is a hybrid of these two philosophies as forged in the fires of my life journey. It is sculpted to be business savvy and facilitate a leader's ability to unleash the high-performance power of any team. I have bolded some of the key words or phrases from each leadership style above that are foundational in TTLO Leadership.

The Parker Principles are based on the belief that any leader can become a Take The Limits Off Leader. Public or private school does not matter. Elite or Non-Elite college, it doesn't matter. Military service or civil service – it just does NOT matter. You, I mean Y-O-U can be a Great Leader. A Great Leader has no limits on what they can accomplish. Their upward mobility - limitless. Their compensation – limitless. Their ability to have a positive impact on people and organizations – limitless.

Tell me, how great a leader would you be if you took off your limits? This is the future we strive for- limitless.

I contend that we all should live a life where we take off the limits . When you start life on a pig and tobacco farm in North Carolina, it's easy to put limits on your dreams and potential.
- I just want to get off the farm…
- I just want to graduate high school…
- I just want to go to college…

All of which would have been great accomplishments for me and probably enough to live a happy and content life. But in reality, this would have been me settling within the comfort of what I viewed as my limits. I believe so strongly in the power and promise of removing limits from life that my wife and I named our company Take The Limits Off.

I hope you enjoy reading this book and it provides you with dozens of "aha" moments, as well as real world leadership strategies that are easy to digest and execute. This book has one real mission, one purpose – to help you Take The Limits Off your career and your life.

Enjoy!!!

Rangers Lead the Way!

Introduction

Over the last decade, I have presented The Parker Principles a myriad of times to groups of all sizes. From small seminars to keynote addresses, these principles resonate and inspire.

But during all these years, The Parker Principles has been no more than exciting presentations and intimate opportunities to educate, share, and connect with people. After each presentation, time and time again, I graciously received the suggestion that I should write this book. I should share more depth and details about my experience, insights, and leadership philosophy. While deep down, I loved the idea that I could actually add value to leaders at any level, I also had fear.

I feared that what was a great live presentation would not translate into a great book. I feared that writing a book would be difficult, time consuming, and require enormous discipline. My focus on improving my leadership skills, taking care of my people, and delivering results for the organization allowed me to hide myself in the job, an excuse to never write this book.

For the last decade, my New Year's Resolution list would always include one consistent resolution:
- Write this book!

Of course, each and every year by the end of January, I would always have another really "good" reason to not write. Then something happened that changed my life forever.

My grandmother died.

The woman who raised me, provided my Christian and ethical foundation, and loved me relentlessly was suddenly gone. Thankfully, I was blessed to spend her last days at her bedside. My grandmother died from kidney failure at 97 years young. I have heard doctors and nurses refer to this a "gentle death," so we had hours and hours to sit and talk. Though my grandmother was born to a sharecropper father and had little more than a high school education, she was by far the smartest person I have ever known. Her mind was sharp and alert to the very end.

We would talk about faith, family, and my career. We had endless conversations about politics. It was during one final conversation that we talked about fighting fear and finding peace with a purpose. We talked about this book and the real reason I have been "writing" it for a decade. We talked about the fear that controlled and sabotaged me in this effort. She reminded me that all of the significant accomplishments I've made in my life were achieved by engaging courage and faith in the face of fear. One of my final promises to this angel of a woman was that I would get this book complete and published within one year. No exceptions.

No Excuses.

She looked straight into my eyes and told me, with courage and faith, I would not only confront my fears, I would also overcome them. So here I am and here we are. Every time I would sit and write, I would pull out her picture and talk to her. I would let her know this book is for her as promised. I live everyday knowing she is with me and watching over me. Each day, I strive to make her proud of the man she helped me become.

While I was determined to face my fear and write this book, I still faced the dilemma of how to translate the subject matter that I can speak so passionately and fearlessly about into a book that reads with the same level of energy and enthusiasm? And not just any book, but a great book that is exciting, authentic, and adds value. How do I convey the emphasis, energy, and expertise without the benefit of voice inflection, hand gestures, or even eye contact? Could I write a book that is easily digested and effectively translates the leadership lessons from my life's journey into something that could actually make a difference in any leader's life?

I needed to convey the energy, sincerity, authenticity, and call to action that comes to me so easily in front of an audience into a book written just for YOU. I want this book to be real for YOU and to give YOU pertinent foundational tools that can change your life and the way you lead.

The Parker Principles is not designed to be a simple how-to, color by numbers manual. It is more of an impetus for you to engage in thought provoking self-reflection on your current leadership style and philosophy. I've learned a great deal in my journey from the farm to the c-suite. I've collected nuggets of information, insights, and critical wisdom along the way that you may find compelling.

While the Parker Principles is the result of my life's journey, joy, sorrow, triumphs and mistakes, the principles are not meant to be all-encompassing or all-knowing. I am not here to speak to you as a professor or a preacher. The Principles are simply the leadership philosophies of an ordinary man with ordinary intellect and talent blessed with an extraordinary career. A man with a fearless commitment to learn, absorb, and adapt to the world in which we are charged to lead.

Through the years, I have excelled at delivering remarkable results regardless role, company, industry, culture, internal issues, or macroeconomic forces. I always focused on the one thing that is constant and completely within my power to control – how I lead. Strength in leadership has been my secret weapon and the "Ace up my Sleeve" during my entire journey. Investing all that I am into being the best leader I can be has paid dividends beyond my wildest dreams. The Parker Principles is designed to share with you the top 10 foundational leadership principles that have worked exceptionally well for me over my career. They are not magic and can be learned, adapted, and adopted.

The Parker Principles: 10 Leadership Force Multipliers

1. Leadership is Learning
2. Build Trust by Leading with Authenticity
3. Courageous Leadership: Dare to Dream and Dare to Fail!
4. Leadership is Relationships: Develop Real Relationships
5. Be a Great Listener
6. Own Your Power: No Excuses!
7. Embrace Humility
8. Believe in Something
9. Be Strong, Fit and Confident
10. Be Enthusiastic and Optimistic

I call these 10 principles, **Leadership Force Multipliers** for a very specific reason. My introduction to the term "force multiplier" reaches back to my military days.

The Department of Defense defines a force multiplier as:

"A capability that, when added to and employed by a combat force, significantly increases the combat potential of that force and thus enhances the probability of successful mission accomplishment."

Corporate world translation:

It is a capability or tool that will magnify or amplify any effort, process, or procedure that will result in increased efficiency, effectiveness, and output.

The example I found most often used to put the concept of force multiplier in to "plain speak" is the hammer. Trying to put a nail in a board with your hand is not only ineffective; it's silly. To solve this issue, you use a tool, a hammer, to amplify the force of your hand on the nail, creating a more effective and efficient system for achieving the desired output –a nail driven into the board.

My vision of **leadership** force multipliers is different. I see tools used as a lever, when properly employed by just one person, can move or change the world.

Each principle, or leadership force multiplier, is a tool that, when properly employed, can move your world. Like with any tool, recognizing the type and purpose of a tool is not enough. There needs to be an innate or learned understanding of how and when to use a tool … let's call it "tool savvy."

You must recognize:
- What tool is needed for the job?
- If the tool is in good working order?
- How the tool works?
- Why this tool works best?
- How to engage the tool to achieve your desired result?

The content of this book will provide you with "tool savvy."

Conceptually, it's simple to recognize and even accept that "Being a Great Listener" is a critical tool to enhance and amplify your leadership, but are you "tool savvy" on "Being a Great Listener"? You will be after reading this book.

The Parker Principles is not intended to be a one-time read.

I suggest that whenever you have a "defining moment" i.e., a job change, promotion, new company, or new macro-economic conditions, you return and review key information in this book again. I am willing to bet you a cup of coffee that you will either find some new insights or will identify best practices you may be employing at less than 100%.

Great Leadership is more magic than science. Like great magic it's amazing, mysterious, impossible, and awe-inspiring...until you start to learn the secrets. Once you start to understand the mechanics, sleight of hand, and best practices behind the magic, then magic becomes less daunting and intimidating. You have the knowledge to make magic manageable and repeatable. You practice, learn, adopt, adapt then practice more. You add your own style and flair to the magic, your own authentic brand of magic. Then one day you wake up and find out you have become a great magician.

You are now the great leader that people want to follow, model, and mentor. You are that great leader that always delivers results and accomplishes the mission. You are that great leader that peers and bosses respect and trust with any critical project or tough assignment. You are that great leader, who knows how to succeed in the right way. YOU are that great leader!. You're amazing, mysterious, and awe-inspiring. You're a magician!

Read on and let's go make some magic!

Parker Principle #1

Leadership is Learning

"Leadership and learning are indispensable to each other."
President John F. Kennedy

A quote from the speech that John F. Kennedy prepared for delivery in Dallas that infamous day in 1963. This is a powerful and clear statement made by one of the most instantly recognizable leaders of our times. Although Parker Principle #1 – Leadership is Learning – may not be as profound or as philosophical as that President Kennedy quote, I believe they both share the same foundational principle that Leadership and Learning are interconnected and interdependent. Time after time, President Kennedy faced one of a kind leadership challenges that reinforced his belief in the connection between Leadership and Learning.

April 12, 1961 – The Soviet cosmonaut Yuri Gagarin becomes the first man in space... catapulting the Soviet Union and their ballistic missile program to a dominant position over the United States in the Superpower Space race.

April 15, 1961 – The U.S. sponsored invasion of Cuba at the Bay of Pigs spectacularly fails due to facing an overwhelming force and inadequate support. The CIA–trained brigade of anti-Castro exiles is completely defeated in just a few days. Kennedy takes responsibility for the disaster.

May 5, 1961 – Alan Sheppard Jr becomes the first American in space, and on May 25, 1961, Kennedy pledges that the U.S. will land a man on the moon before the end of the decade.

August 13, 1961 – After failing to resolve the longstanding conflict in a meeting with Nikita Khrushchev, the East Germans supported by the Soviet Union begin construction of the Berlin Wall. This marked a physical incarnation of the Iron Curtain and cemented the de facto positions of the Superpowers for the Cold War.

October 22, 1962 – Kennedy announces to the American people that the Soviet Union was building offensive missile sites in Cuba solely to provide them with nuclear strike capability against the Western Hemisphere. He stated he would protect the United States against such a threat no matter what the cost and would impose a naval blockade and quarantine around Cuba. The world was on the brink of a Global nuclear war and likely nuclear holocaust.

These significant leadership defining events were so singular and epic in scale and scope that no amount of experience alone could have prepared any leader to handle them. But Kennedy considered himself a learning leader, and I believe it was his commitment to a learning leader philosophy that helped him handle these situations and be considered by history as one of the greatest American Presidents.

I have read a significant amount of material that hotly debates whether leadership is an innate or acquired ability. I'm not here to support either position, but I do have a position. I'm sure some leadership abilities are innate. I also believe great leaders demonstrate an intricate combination of innate qualities and abilities along with those that have been acquired or enhanced by learning.

> *"Live as if you were to die tomorrow. Learn as if you were to live forever."*
> **Mahatma Gandhi**

Leadership is Learning

This is the foundational **cornerstone** of my view and success as a leader. My use of the word cornerstone is purposeful and has a specific meaning. The cornerstone concept is derived from the first stone set in the construction of a foundation. It is the most critical stone of the entire construction and of significance because all other stones will be set in reference to this stone, thus determining the position of the entire structure. For my structure of great leadership, learning is the **cornerstone**.

Today's leaders, especially at the senior level, could not have achieved their position without having some level of commitment to the preparation and dedication needed to maintain that position. These leaders are eager to update their perspective on the world and business in an effort to anticipate what is waiting for them, their teams and their organization just over the horizon. The skillset required to enhance a leader's ability to "view over the horizon" is directly affected by that leaders' ability and willingness to learn.

Do you VUCA?

In the late 1990's, the US Army coined the acronym V.U.C.A., pronounced "VooKah", to depict the radically different military threats that arise when conditions are 'Volatile, Uncertain, Complex and Ambiguous.' But it was not until the terrorist attacks of September 11, 2001 that the notion and acronym successfully transitioned into the business environment. VUCA has been adopted by strategic business leaders to describe the chaotic, turbulent, and rapidly changing business environment that has become accepted as the "new normal."

The VUCA construct can neatly encapsulate the turbulent and unpredictable nature of today's business environment. I deliver Keynotes, Seminars, and Workshops specifically dedicated to preparing leaders, teams, and organizations to succeed in a VUCA world. I will lightly touch on VUCA in business and the importance of learning in VUCA Leadership.

Volatility. The nature, speed, volume, and magnitude of change that is not in a predictable pattern - Global competition, disruptive technologies, interconnectivity, social media, turbulent financial markets, and digitization have made business markets more chaotic and increasingly unstable.

Uncertainty. This is simply the lack of predictability in issues and events in the business world. Forecasting the future has become more difficult than ever, as past issues and events are no longer accurate predictors of future outcomes.

Complexity*.* This is simply the recognition and acknowledgement that there are often numerous and difficult to understand causes, interdependent variables, and mitigating factors – both inside and outside an organization involved in a problem or crisis.

Ambiguity*.* The lack of clarity about the meaning of an event or action that translates into an inability to conceptualize threats and opportunities accurately before they become erosive. These events and actions are open to multiple interpretations possibly obscuring marketplace and company dynamics that dramatically increase the potential for misreads, mixed meanings, and mistakes.

It has always been the traditional role of a leader to anticipate change, identify opportunities, create strategic plans, motivate and direct people, manage risks, solve problems, and make effective decisions. In a VUCA construct, these tasks are made more difficult. A VUCA world demands a different type of leadership style to succeed. VUCA leaders and successful VUCA leadership will be determined by the leader and their organization's ability and commitment to learn. Let me introduce you to VUCA Prime – developed by Bob Johansen, a distinguished fellow at the Institute for the Future. The goal of VUCA Prime is to help organizations identify what characteristics are found in the best VUCA leaders and what characteristics must be learned by all leaders to succeed in a VUCA world. VUCA Prime categories of Vision, Understanding, Clarity, and Agility are specifically designed to counter each aspect of VUCA.

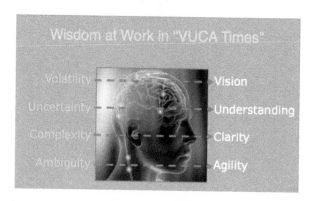

VUCA Leaders must become VUCA Learners.

Volatility is countered by **Vision** – It is a fact that these are turbulent times, and leaders with a clear vision of where they want their organization to go in the next year, three years, and five years will be better positioned to weather volatile business changes, such as economic downturns or new competition in their markets.

Uncertainty is countered by **Understanding** – While the concept of gaining Understanding is simple to "understand," it is a complex strategy to execute. The best method I have found for leaders to increase their understanding is SL^3 (Stop, Look, Listen and Learn). SL^3 requires leaders to engage their own self-awareness and humility to reach out beyond their normal functional areas and comfort zones. Leaders must sharpen their skills in communication, collaboration, teamwork, and culture dynamics to engage employees at all levels in the organization.

Complexity is countered by **Clarity** – Finding Clarity requires leaders to execute deliberate processes and best practices focused on trying to make sense of the chaos. Being a VUCA leader means accepting as fact that the world is filled with chaos and it comes fast and furious. VUCA leaders who can expeditiously and precisely assimilate, prioritize, and triage the minutiae associated with chaos will make superior business decisions.

Ambiguity is countered by **Agility** – Agility is achieved when a Leader can engage the qualities and processes of "agile leadership" and guide their teams and organizations to a place where business agility is a cultural norm. The Agile leader must hone and augment their savvy and expertise in communication, intellectual curiosity, trust, commitment, inspiration, innovation and risk taking. An organization must have agile leaders to achieve a culture of Agility.

The VUCA Prime elements of Vision, Understanding, Clarity, and Agility are not meant to be mutually exclusive but mutually supportive. Each one should intertwine with the singular purpose of helping any leader become a robust VUCA learner, a trait that works to accelerate the individual's transformation into a tenacious VUCA leader.

This VUCA leader will approach the world with a fresh mindset and the ability to adopt a new process or behavior consistent with the current business situation in the VUCA world.

15

This VUCA leader will be able to deploy a new array of skills that will give them the strategic and competitive advantage in the VUCA world: Communication, Teamwork, Collaboration, Information Gathering, Data Analysis, Empowerment, Agility and Strategic Thinking Skills.

If you can accept the premise that this is a VUCA world that can be best addressed by VUCA leaders, then you can also accept the overwhelming need for any organization to be a learning organization.

> *"Learning is not attained by chance. It must be sought for with ardor and attended to with diligence."*
> **Abigail Adams**

It has been my experience that the *Best Leaders* are consistently the *Best Learners*. Today's leader must be comfortable living in a state of continual evolution. In a time when most skills have a half-life of about five years, a leader must shoulder the responsibility of reinvention and relevance. They must constantly renew their perspective to secure the success of their teams and organizations. These leaders not only need to master swift, relevant, and autonomous learning, but they also must be the most vigorous supporter and promoter of learning within their organization.

In a recent Deloitte study, Global Human Capital Trends 2017, 83% of the respondents identified learning as being important or very important. Of the 10 human capital trends cited by global human resource leaders as areas where organizations needed to close the gap between the pace of change and talent management, learning ranked #2 in importance, just three percentage points behind Building the Organization of the Future. While Learning was ranked #2 in importance, according to the study, more companies than ever report they are unprepared to address this challenge.

I believe, because you are here with me right now, reading this book, you are a leader that understands what the Deloitte study confirms. Learning is of critical importance to both your individual success as a leader and the overall success of your organization. There has to be a strong sense of personal commitment to learning, especially after you have achieved a position of power and responsibility. This brings us to two of the most important questions you should ask yourself: Are you learning as fast as the world is changing? Is your organization?

If your answer to both questions is not a loud and confident "Hell Yes!", then you should be thinking about establishing an individual and organizational learning strategy.

> *"I am always ready to learn although I do not always like being taught."*
> **Winston Churchill**

Let's focus on your individual learning strategy. Is it the learning strategy of a great leader? Earlier, I took the position that leadership is an undetermined but individual composition of both innate and acquired abilities. The magic of learning is that it's dual purposed. Not only will learning allow you to acquire new abilities, but it will also enable you to take the limits off your innate abilities. Learning will allow you to unleash your full leadership potential and efficacy. As you create your individual learning strategy, remember every leader has a need for constant evolution.

Developing an effective learning strategy means you should:

- Dedicate yourself to a "never stop learning" philosophy. Learning is a lifelong endeavor because life never stops teaching.

- Strive to become a more self-aware, conscious, and empathetic leader. This will allow you to understand yourself and your team. This understanding will enable you to recognize the team's needs, motivations, and strengths as you learn to leverage your own intrinsic traits to serve your team best.

- Include Mentorship – If Leadership is a craft, then you must be able to teach a craft to Master it.

- Engage peers and experts in your function and industry as learning resources.

- Identify and list the top 15 skills or characteristics that you believe reflect your authentic leadership style. I call this my ultimate take the limits off list or **TTLO-15**.

- The end state goal is to develop a specific learning strategy for each of your **TTLO-15**. Once you have your TTLO-15, start to execute a realistic triage phase. The triage phase is simply prioritizing the **TTLO-15** into three distinct buckets (5-5-5)– Critical, Important, and Aspirational. My advice, be true to the triage and force ranking of your **TTLO-15**. Leaders usually have the most angst in deciding what 5 will go into the Aspirational bucket. This force ranking will help dictate the order in which you develop and resource your 15 learning strategies.

In my process, I also use predetermined "inflection points" that require me to review, evaluate, update, and validate the TTLO-15 and their assigned triage buckets. I use 2 categories of inflection points: Professional and Personal.

- Professional Inflection Points – These points can include a variety of factors, such as a new role, new boss, new team, competitive marketplace disruption, and internal or external crisis.

- Personal Inflection Points – These run similar to a health insurance "qualifying event"- marriage, divorce, birth, adoption, immediate family death etc. You may be surprised how much of an effect a personal inflection point may have on our perspectives and priorities.

In no special order, here is my TTLO-15:
- Trust
- Communication
- Empathy
- Integrity
- Mission Accomplishment(results)
- Confidence/Strength
- Stability
- Energy/Passion
- Authenticity
- Inspiration

- Decisiveness
- Accountability
- Perseverance
- Innovation
- Intellectual Curiosity
- PUT IN THE WORK! – every day

"The purpose of learning is growth, and our minds, unlike our bodies, can continue growing as we continue to live."
Mortimer Adler

Now, this next section may be slightly controversial, but we are talking about the power of learning as a leadership force multiplier. All I ask is that you read the next section with an open mind then take a little time over the next couple of days to engage in some deep reflection on this before you decide whether to accept or dismiss this section.

Intellectual Curiosity should be one of the top 5 – Go or NO GO criteria for hiring, retaining, and training talent for your organization. Some business situations could bump this up to a top 3 criteria. That's just plain crazy, right? Maybe you glanced back at my TTLO-15(or you are referencing your own) and you are thinking of 7,8 or 14 of them that would rank above intellectual curiosity in your talent management decision. Just a reminder – open mind then reflection, please.

"A man who asks is a fool for five minutes. A man who never asks is a fool for life."
Chinese Proverb

As leaders, when we recruit leadership talent from outside the organization, or investigate bringing an internal leadership candidate onto a team, we usually have very specific qualities, experience, behavioral competencies, and personal characteristics that we know will increase the new leader's chance for success. While we may have more than a dozen clear cut requirements that we would like a new leader to possess, there is usually a Top 5 that we deem the candidate must have - period. In the last 5 to 10 years, Intellectual Curiosity has become one of my Top 5. The more senior the role, the more critical Intellectual Curiosity is to a leader's ability to succeed. I have rejected candidates that have checked every box on the role requirements list but came up short in Intellectual Curiosity. Frankly, I would expect to be rejected as a candidate for any senior leadership role if I did not clearly convey Intellectual Curiosity as one of the key strengths I bring to the table.

First, I want to make sure you do not confuse Intellectual Curiosity with Intelligence. While they accompany each other in most leaders, that is not always the case.

Intelligence is usually defined as *the ability to learn* or understand or deal with new or trying situations. This ability is often referenced and quantified as a person's (**IQ – Intelligence Quotient**). *Intellectual Curiosity* is consistently defined as one's deep and persistent **desire to know**: one's **desire to** invest time and energy into **learning** more about a person, place, thing, or concept. I have seen this desire quantified as a person's (**CQ- Curiosity Quotient**). **IQ** is *the ability* to learn and **CQ** is *the desire* to learn. I always equate **IQ** horsepower as an important asset for any leader but having intelligence without curiosity is like having the innate **ability** to be an Olympic athlete without the **desire** to put in the training and work. Final verdict, if you don't put in the work, then "you won't" become an Olympic athlete. Deal Breaker!

> *"The greatest enemy of learning is knowing."*
> **John Maxwell**

Let's get back to the business aspect of Intellectual Curiosity. There are two real world substantive reasons to hire for Intellectual Curiosity – 1) It's a VUCA world, and 2) they make the best leaders and employees.

It's a VUCA world – earlier we talked about the leadership needs and requirements for an organization to succeed in a VUCA (**V**olatile, **U**ncertain, **C**omplex, **A**mbiguous) world. Leaders with strong Intellectual Curiosity make the best VUCA leaders. Leaders with high **CQ's** tend to have the key characteristics needed to lead in a VUCA world.

They:
- Learn and Adapt Faster- (**V, A**)
- Listen and Engage Better- (**U, A**)
- Bring in New Knowledge and Ideas – (**U, C, A**)
- Foster Openness in Discourse, Driving Innovation – (**U, C**)

- Sponsor Smart Risk Taking and Learn from Failure – **(V, U, C, A)**
- Leverage High Performance Networks- Inside and Outside their Industry – **(U, C, A)**

Throughout my career, the Best Leaders have consistently been the Best Learners, and learning is driven by high **CQ**. I've also seen leaders with high **CQ's** tend to have empathy and seek to surround themselves with diversity of culture and of thinking. They leverage both the power and the science of "why" and sponsor an open and curious culture grounded in the desire to learn. An organization with a culture of learning attracts and retains intellectually curious employees. These employees tend to be faster learners and are willing to invest the time and energy to expand their learning. They also tend to be extremely engaged in their organization and the world around them; they pride themselves on being innovative and forward thinking.

"Learn everything you can, anytime you can, from anyone you can - there will always come a time when you will be grateful you did".
Sarah Caldwell

My final note on Intellectual Curiosity – I recommend you create and execute a strategy to recruit, retain, and train for Intellectual Curiosity in all levels of your organization.

Hiring High CQ Talent:

When I interview a candidate, I am always testing and looking for high **CQ's**. While I wish there was an exact science to testing and recognizing high CQ in a candidate, there is not. It is more like you know it when you see it vs a mathematical formula. That being said, there are some simple tools anyone can use to investigate a candidate's CQ.

1. Ask the right questions:

    a. Tell me about something you have taught yourself in the last six months? What process did you use ? Were you successful?

b. What is the most interesting book you have read in the last six months? Why did you find it interesting?

c. What interests you about our organization? What advice would you give me?

d. What would you like to be doing here in the next 3 to 5 years?

e. What do you see as the organization's biggest challenge over the next 3 to 5 years?

These questions will give you some insight into the candidate's curiosity, their ability to research, and their ability to think and be curious beyond the role for which they are interviewing.

2. Give them Pre-Interview projects – I adopted this from a Search Executive when we were looking for the CEO of the company where I serve on the Board of Directors. She sent each candidate a questionnaire to complete that contained questions that tested their level of CQ. Over the years, I've adapted the questionnaire to be a pre-interview project that the candidate would bring to the interview. I usually reserve this only for finalists. For example, bring in a "blog submission" about our latest commercial, ad campaign, new product, or acquisition.

3. Evaluate the Candidate's Questions

a. Carefully listen to and evaluate the questions the candidate asks for both quantity and quality. Is it a well thought out, thoroughly researched original question that you have to engage your brain actively to answer? Or is it one of those canned questions that you get when you Google "List of Questions to Ask at the end of an Interview." Please don't misunderstand; there are some really good questions on some of these lists but when you only get one or two questions and one of those is "What does a typical day in the role look like?" Deal Breaker.

Retaining High CQ Talent

High CQ talent tend to fight both the status quo and a closed and non-transparent culture. There are very specific steps you can take to help retain high CQ employees.

1. Hire high CQ leaders – they promote an environment and culture of openness, constructive debate, and transparency. They like to involve as many big brains as viable in the strategy and decision-making process.

2. Reinforce learning as a core value and sponsor both formal and informal learning opportunities.

3. Increase opportunities for employees to work on task forces and project teams outside their everyday job to expand the scope of their world.

4. Sponsor an informal mentorship program that will allow high CQ employees to gain insights and understanding beyond their current role.

5. Create a reward and compensation system that includes learning as a variable.

6. Create an environment where smart, well-researched risk taking is rewarded… even if it ends in failure.

7. Adopt the concept of After Action Reviews (AARs) – I was introduced and immersed in the concept and practice of the After Action Review while in the military.

    AAR's were a critical and mandated part of life in the 82nd Airborne Division and U.S. Army Ranger School. For the military, it's simply a highly structured process to help provide soldiers and units feedback on mission and task performances in training and in combat. AAR's identify how to correct deficiencies, sustain strengths, and focus on the performance of the specific mission. I continued to use and adopted the AAR process in my corporate career. Instead of a review after training or combat operations, it became a review at the end of a negative event or customer loss.

While I maintained strict adherence to the AAR construct and design, I initially implemented modifications to "de-militarize" the process and make it more corporate friendly – initially calling it a PMR (post-mortem review). After a while, I abandoned the "post-mortem" name and went back to AARs for three specific reasons. First, Post-Mortem sounds a little morbid. Second, the PMR process became a negative, thinly disguised blame game. Third and most important, the PMR negative connotation limited the process to be viewed as a tool that should only be utilized after a negative event – loss of a customer, loss of an RFP, a bad press event, natural disaster...

In my view, this severely underutilized the process and significantly limited it from achieving its full potential as a powerful learning tool. In a learning organization, learning tools should be a part of everyday life, not just during times of loss or negative actions. I found it was just as important to do AARs after an RFP or new customer win as it was after a loss. The same AAR is needed, whether you have a commercial or ad campaign that was a huge success or when you have one that flops.

The AAR process consists of four distinct parts:

1.   Planning the AAR
   - Who will run the AAR?
   - Who will attend?
   - What are the logistical details?
   - What outside support or resources should be engaged?
2.   Preparing for the AAR
   - Gather all relevant information, validate facts, confirm details.
   - Designate a scribe.
   - Gather external information and points of view.
3.   Conducting the AAR
   - Introduction and Housekeeping.

- o Validate Objectives (Answer the 4 Basic Questions)
  - What was expected to happen?
  - What actually happened?
  - What went well and why?
  - What can be improved and how?
- o Rules of Engagement.
  - Participation by everyone in attendance is mandatory.
  - Must have an open, honest and respectful discussion.
  - Focus on the results of the event, program, or project.
  - Identify ways to sustain or repeat what was done well.
  - Develop recommendations on how to change, improve, or overcome obstacles and challenges.
- o Meeting Summary by AAR leader and next steps

4. AAR Follow Up.
  - o The AAR leader ensures the results of the AAR are shared with senior leadership, then with the entire organization.

"In a time of drastic change, it is the learners who inherit the future. The learned usually find themselves equipped to live in a world that no longer exists".
Eric Hoffer

Leadership is Learning and Learning is Life and Life Never Stops Teaching.

I know I have put a lot of content in this chapter. The exciting part is this is just the beginning. Leadership is Learning - is my first leadership Multiplier chapter by design. Learning and the willingness to learn will be the cornerstone with which you will build your personal leadership architecture and style.

The concept of learning is one I hold near and dear to my heart. Caught up in the maddening speed of business, we sometimes forget we are students of life and it continually provides learning opportunities. However, it is up to each of us to expand on those opportunities by ferociously seeking knowledge throughout each day. With that in mind, I challenge you to read everything relevant to your own personal craft and your position.

Trust me when I say I am not asking you to do anything that I would not, and do not, do myself. Each day, I invest time and energy learning and developing my craft. After all, this is not simply a professional journey, but a personal one.

Not sure where to start? I can understand that. After all, there are literally thousands of great books out there just waiting to be cracked open. So here are a few of my favorites to help you get started:

It Worked for Me: In Life and Leadership – Colin Powell
Straight from the Gut – Jack Welch
Good to Great – Jim Collins
7 Habits of Highly Effective People – Stephen Covey
First Break all the Rules – Marcus Buckingham
Now Discover Your Strengths – Marcus Buckingham
5 Levels of Leadership – John Maxwell
Developing the Leader Within – John Maxwell
21 Indispensable Qualities of a Leader – John Maxwell
The First 90 Days – Michael Watkins

Right now, you might be thinking…that's A LOT of knowledge! And you would be right. But the real question is, **how do you use it?**

These books contain a lot of information to digest. It can be daunting and even overwhelming. So, my advice is to read, analyze, and then decide what parts align with your authentic self and style. Maybe only 20% does. Take that information, put it on your tool belt, and use it immediately. Take the remaining 80% and put it in your tool box for later use. As your style matures and evolves, you will find items that resonated early in your career will fade as you continue to grow, while others that don't speak as loudly to you originally will become more relevant later.

"Here is one additional resource to consider." One of the biggest learning mistakes I see people make is that they fail to take advantage of the development resources offered by their current employer. If your organization offers courses or training in leadership, professional development, presentation skills, or even in the form of a 360-degree feedback, then I encourage you to take advantage of that process and use it to build your own skill set.

I would like to leave you with a few parting thoughts.

There is no other single action you can engage in to take the limits off your leadership potential than ferocious learning.

Have belief in your ability to learn, invest the time and energy in yourself to learn, and dedicate yourself to the mission of learning.

Prepare yourself for the VUCA world and surround yourself with a high CQ team

"Tell me and I forget. Teach me and I remember. Involve me and I learn."
Benjamin Franklin

If leadership is your craft, then seek to be a Master of your craft, understanding that true Masters are lifelong students and the only way to true mastery is through teaching. Find someone (inside or outside your organization) with high potential and high CQ and mentor them. It will make you both better leaders.

"There is no end to education. It is not that you read a book, pass an examination, and finish with education. The whole of life, from the moment you are born to the moment you die, is a process of learning."
Jiddu Krishnamurti

Last, never forget the learning derived from taking the time for real introspection. We develop wisdom and drive true and lasting change in our daily behavior through the process of applying what we have learned and reflecting on our personal experiences.

Leadership is Learning
Chapter Recap

- Learning is the Cornerstone for building your Leadership structure.
- The new normal for business chaos is V.U.C.A. It is a **V**olatile, **U**ncertain, **C**omplex, and **A**mbiguous world.
- Use VUCA Prime to combat business chaos – Vision vs Volatility, Understanding vs Uncertainty, Clarity vs Complexity and Agility vs Ambiguity.
- What is your TTLO-15? The 15 skills or characteristics that you believe reflect your authentic leadership style.
- Hire, train, and retain Intellectual Curiosity (CQ).
- Implement a disciplined, structured, and consistent After Action Review (AAR) process.
- Put in the work to learn, develop, and grow every day.
- Put new leadership knowledge on your tool belt to use today or in your tool box to use in the future.
- Remember the learning derived from honest introspection.
- Leadership is Learning, Learning is Life, and Life Never Stops Teaching.

Parker Principle #2

Build Trust by Leading with Authenticity

"The glue that holds all relationships together--including the relationship between the leader and the led--is trust, and trust is based on integrity."
Brian Tracy

This is one of my favorite quotes that clearly conceptualizes an intimate relationship based on mutual trust between those who lead and those who follow. There is no way around it; people will not follow you if they don't trust you. It doesn't matter how much intelligence, charisma, experience, or skillset you possess. You will not be a great leader, not even a good leader, if your team does NOT trust you. The trust relationship between you and your team is one of the most important relationships you will ever have outside of family or religion.

Trust is the tenuous interpersonal link between leaders and followers. It is the fundamental belief that, as a follower, I can rely on my leader's actions, words, and intentions. That my leader will try to deliver on their commitments and that they have "some" consideration for my best interest. Trust is critically important because, as the follower, I am vulnerable to those actions, words, and intentions. As the follower, I don't possess the status, position level, or power of the leader, so I have more risk and exposure than the leader. If I have that risk, then my family shares that risk. We have all been followers throughout our careers, so we recognize and understand that sense of vulnerability and sometimes helplessness to the desires, emotions, and decisions of our leaders. I have been blessed to work for many great leaders throughout my career. I have also been blessed to work for a few terrible ones.

I know that sounds weird. How could both great and terrible leaders be a blessing? The great leaders validated the characteristics and behaviors of the leader I aspire to be. The terrible leaders demonstrated and substantiated the implications and impact of the leader I refuse to be. While I can name a dozen important leadership characteristics that differentiated the great leaders from the terrible ones, if I am honest with myself, it boiled down to one differentiator that mattered – Trust.

Trust above all else. All the great leaders I trusted and the terrible ones I did not. With the great leaders, I trusted their actions, words, and intentions. I trusted that, if I delivered stellar results for them, with integrity, loyalty and commitment, these leaders would be invested in my best interest. With the terrible leaders, no matter what I delivered or how I delivered it, I never felt secure in my job. I was always waiting for the "other shoe to drop." I always suspected that the positive praise that they used with me in private did not match how they viewed or discussed me with others. They were never invested in me, my career, or my family. No trust. If you have been around long enough – you've had that terrible boss. You may have that boss right now.

My recommendation is that, if you have a leader you don't trust – find a new one. Whether you go to another team or to another organization, just go. If you don't trust your leader, you've probably been contemplating and dreaming about leaving. You are probably miserable and not bringing 100% of yourself to work every day. You are either on cruise control or hiding out in a bomb shelter trying to make it through the day. Unfortunately, this is a risky strategy. Sooner or later, you will be exposed; someone unexpected will notice the cruising or the hiding – like your boss, your boss's boss, your peers, the people you lead… They will notice and take note. It will negatively affect your reputation and their perception of you. Then the unthinkable, you wake up one day and find yourself expendable. If that isn't enough to galvanize you into action, how about this? We spend most of our waking adult lives at work, and life is way too short to be miserable or hiding every day.

I don't think any of us wake up in the morning, look in the mirror, and decide to be that terrible distrusted leader, whose most talented people are leaving, hiding, or not bringing 100% of themselves to work every day. The good news, while the competition, marketplace, or macroeconomic situation may not be in your power to control, trust and being a trusted leader is within your power. Are you a trusted leader? Are you leading in a trusted organization? Are you engaging in the right activities to inspire and build trust with your team. Are you building trust through character and authenticity?

"Leadership requires five ingredients--brains, energy, determination, trust, and ethics. The key challenges today are in terms of the last two--trust and ethics. "
Fred Hilmer

Trusted Leadership

Before we dive into the trust building power of Authentic Leadership, let's talk about trust. Trust seems to be in serious decline or even historic lows in our world today. This is an across the spectrum phenomena – our Big Business, Media, Criminal Justice System, Healthcare, Public Schools, Government, Banks ..., trust erosion is widespread and intensifying. A quick note, you will see me use both mistrust and distrust interchangeably, and just to clarify, because I had to research it myself, distrust and mistrust basically mean the same thing as a verb... "to be without **confidence**" and as a noun... "lack of trust or **confidence**." In either case, it is "to be without" or "a lack of" **confidence**.

The most recent trust Gallup Poll looking at the Confidence in Institutions (Sep 2016) asked the simple question:

How much confidence do you have in each institution?
- a great deal
- quite a lot
- some
- very little

The poll measures a positive trust score as the combination of "a great deal + quite a lot." In this survey, positive trust scores range from a high with The Military of 73% to a low with the Congress at 9%. No, that is not a misprint; only 9% of the respondents have a great deal or quite a lot of trust for Congress. Wow!

As a business leader, I wanted to understand the business dynamic. The survey shows Small Business at 68% and Big Business at 18% (Congress is the only lower rated institution). Believe it or not, that is good news; if you are a leader in a small business (generally 1000 or less employees), then you have a great foundation to build even more trust at 68%. For all other business leaders, a trust factor of 18% is alarming.

31

This poll surveyed 15 disparate institutions with the most trusted being The Military, Small Business, The Police, The Church and The Medical System and the least trusted being The Criminal Justice System, Television News, Newspapers, Big Business, and Congress.

I am going to read you a list of institutions in American society. Please tell me how much confidence you, yourself, have in each one – a great deal, quite a lot, some or very little?[1]

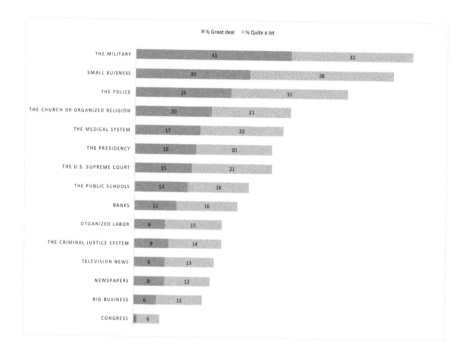

Even more troubling than the dramatic range in the scores, through June 2016, all institutions, with the exceptions of Small Business and The Presidency, are showing trust declines from their high points in the last decade.

Insittution	Jun-16	10yr High	(+/-)10yr High
The Military	73	82	-9
Small Business	68	67	1
The Police	56	59	-3
The Church	41	52	-11
The Medical System	39	41	-2
The Presidency	36	33	3
The U.S. Supreme Court	36	39	-3
The Public Schools	30	38	-8
Banks	27	49	-22
Organized Labor	23	24	-1
The Criminal Justice System	23	29	-6
Television News	21	31	-10
Newspapers	20	30	-10
Big Business	20	30	-10
Congress	9	19	-10

So, I feel confident in the statement that Trust or the lack thereof is a serious challenge, and that may be an understatement. In my research, I have seen this called a trust crisis, a trust meltdown, and even a distrust tsunami. It doesn't matter what name you give it; the decline in trust represents one of the most significant challenges facing leaders today.

To most leaders, this trust challenge is alarming, intimidating, and discouraging. We know distrust has a negative impact on our business, but it's tough to get our arms around the importance to take action around trust. What actions do we take and how much of our resources do we allocate to these actions? Trust in business is relational, abstract, and tough to measure or quantify.

"Think about it this way: When trust is low, in a company or in a relationship, it places a hidden "tax" on every transaction: every communication, every interaction, every strategy, every decision is taxed, bringing speed down and sending costs up. My experience is that significant distrust doubles the cost of doing business and triples the time it takes to get things done.

By contrast, individuals and organizations that have earned and operate with high trust experience the opposite of a tax -- a "dividend" that is like a performance multiplier, enabling them to succeed in their communications, interactions, and decisions, and to move with incredible speed. A recent Watson Wyatt study showed that high trust companies outperform low trust companies by nearly 300%!"
Stephen M.R. Covey
Author The Speed of Trust

As a leader, you are tasked to deliver great results by building and leading high-performance teams. You must lead with vision, purpose, effective communication, strategic agility, innovation, passion, foresight, and many other abilities. But if your team or organization does not trust you, all those great leadership abilities are obstructed and incapacitated.

There is tremendous data that consistently reaffirms the overwhelming competitive and marketplace advantages attributed to high trust organizations.

High Trust organizations have higher/better:
- Productivity, Revenue Generation and Profit Growth
- Morale, Talent Recruitment and Retention
- Customer Service and Retention
- Communication, Agility and Innovation
- Diversity and Teamwork
- Change Management

This is today's leadership quandary; leaders need to build a high trust organization in a low trust world. Today's leader has to determine the best courses of action to engage and counteract the rising wave of distrust. This is the reality we face: the wave is real, and it will undermine our ability to lead. So, what do we do? We get to work!

> *"Trust is something that is difficult to establish. It is very fragile that needs to be taken care of.*
> *Once trust breaks or shatters into pieces, it is very difficult to rebuild it."*
> **K. Cunningham**

As leaders, to engage, survive, and thrive against the distrust tsunami, we need to prepare like a master surfer. We must understand and recognize the danger signs and then employ the right best practices to build trust. Our simple mission: be a trusted leader that builds a high trust organization. Let's get to work.

Recognize and Understand the Danger Signs of Distrust:

What is the level of trust in your leadership? What is level of trust in your organization? Are you a trusted leader in a high trust organization? Just because you are in charge doesn't mean you are trusted and just because you are a trusted leader doesn't mean you lead a high trust organization.

To answer these questions, you must embark on a trust assessment journey. For this journey, you will need a journal. For the next 30 days, focus on your powers of observation and intuition. Look for the **danger signs** of mistrust and record each sighting in detail in your journal. After 30 days, set aside some time to reflect, review, and consolidate all the journal entries. If you stayed true to the assessment with vigilance and honesty, then believe whatever story your entries are telling you. Let's talk about the 30-day trust assessment. Where do you look and what signs do you look for?

Meetings: This is especially important when you are new to a company, role, or team. You can look for these signs in every type of meeting, but they are extremely important to identify in meetings that include both the leadership and the workforce, where the purpose is to discuss current performance or future strategy of the organization.

- Is leadership fully transparent on the current and future state of the organization or do they withhold information to create a positive "spin"?
- Is leadership too optimistic about their own individual (or their teams') performance and not owning less than optimal results?
- Are leaders providing realistic, open, and accurate opinions and analysis on the organizations strengths, weakness, opportunities, and threats?
- What is the body language in the room? Leaders? Presenters? Audience?
  - Leader/Presenter Low Trust Body Language
    - Hands – hiding, clasping, or wringing indicates insincerity or lack of confidence or belief in what they are saying.
    - Crossed arms – a defensive posture – they are not enthusiastic or confident in the information being presented. The leader feels threatened and the message to the audience is: I am closed and not open to conversation, dialogue or debate on what is being presented.
    - Poor audience eye contact – conveys the leader is insecure, insincere, or that they are hiding something.
  - Audience Low Trust Body Language
    - Crossed arms – defensive – feels threatened by what the leader is saying or doing.
    - Touching or slightly rubbing nose or eye – indicates rejection or doubt in the leader's message.
    - Heads resting in hands, eyes downcast – indicates boredom or lack of engagement.
    - Looking down or face turned away – shows doubt and disbelief in what is being presented.

I would suggest you look for these signs in all meetings – town halls, team meetings, and even one on ones. If you observe these mistrust danger signs, write it down. These are pretty straightforward signs about the level of trust in the leader (including you) and in your organization.

Lack of Courage: When leaders display a lack of courage, it not only significantly diminishes trust, but it's contagious. Lack of courage danger signs include:

- Leaders that don't stand up for what they believe – even when it may be unpopular. If your team cannot predict the way their leader will react or make a decision in a situation, based on that leader's understood or stated core values – they will not trust that leader.
- Leaders that do not openly and transparently face their problems
- Leaders that are afraid to discipline or engage in tough coaching or counseling situations
- Leaders that refuse to make hard or unpopular decisions

> *"A cowardly leader is the most dangerous of men."*
> **Stephen King**

Mean, Backstabbing, and Betrayal Behaviors: I know this seems like one of those "no duh" obvious danger signs, but you would be surprised, maybe even horrified, at how many times I have seen this from leaders. Just to be transparent, I never trusted those leaders again.

- Leaders that badmouth their direct reports, peers, or superiors – I have seen many leaders engage in this practice, predominantly in "non-business and after hours" settings. Sometimes alcohol enabled. It does not matter. My only thought was that if you will say that about "Bill" when they are not around, my goodness what must you be saying about me.
- Leaders that engage in disparagement or belittle a team member's abilities, quirks or misfortune, especially when they try to disguise it as humor or harmless sarcasm
- Leaders who betray confidence-. They are not only destructive to trust, but word spreads about the betrayal, their stature and respect are diminished, and they lose the moral high ground to lead.
- Leaders with hidden agendas

"Sometimes the person you'd take a bullet for is the person behind the trigger."
Taylor Swift

Avoidance and Fear: This can cover a wide range of behaviors, but it all boils down to some level of abdication of leadership responsibilities to embrace some form of hiding.

- Leaders that avoid taking a critical but tough assignment due to risk of not succeeding
- Leaders that consistently avoid conflict and conflict resolution for their teams.
- Leaders that avoid making a decision by hiding behind data, analysis paralysis, "not the right time" or "getting ready". This is sign of fear. We all have fear; we are human but when a leader fails to control and mange that fear – they make fearful decisions, and that fear infects the whole organization.
- Leaders that avoid accountability by always finding someone or something else to blame
- Leaders that only want to hear and will only accept information and opinions that validate their predetermined thoughts and beliefs
- Leaders that hide behind their title, position, or power and must be "right" in all circumstances. They lack humility, grace, or gratitude. They send a clear message that their self-interest is the most important objective. They are determined to be perceived as the smartest person in the room. You know exactly the person I am talking about. It's misguided to think this is just a harmless big ego. It's not; it's fear. Fear of being found out that they are not as strong, intelligent, or competent as they imagine they should be.

"A boss creates fear, a leader confidence. A boss fixes blame, a leader corrects mistakes. A boss knows all, a leader asks questions. A boss makes work drudgery, a leader makes it interesting. A boss is interested in himself or herself, a leader is interested in the group"
Russell H. Ewing

If you are observing any of the above signs, your warning lights should be flashing. If at the end of the assessment you have recorded multiple

38

instances of multiple mistrust signs, you have a trust issue. The weighting of the instances will help you identify the source and build a plan to counteract the distrust. As a leader, you must not only understand the implications of these signs but own the responsibility to take the necessary actions to build credibility and inspire trust. We will talk about some very specific activities and best practices that you, as the leader, can start today. Trust is not magic, but it is magical in its ability to take the limits of your leadership and your organization. Together, we have a simple mission, to be more trusted leaders and build high trust organizations.

"Contrary to what most people believe, trust is not some soft, illusive quality that you either have or you don't; rather, trust is a pragmatic, tangible, actionable asset that you can create."
Stephen R Covey

Building and sustaining Leadership Trust is a delicate, daunting, and formidable endeavor. The leader must make a commitment to the time, energy, perseverance, and character needed to undertake this mission. The good news is that you already possess an instinctual understanding of what that a trusted leader "looks and feels like." I want to provide you with some foundational qualities and characteristics you can use right now to build more trust in your leadership and organization. Overall, there have been 5 that I have observed and correlated with the most trusted leaders operating in high trust organizations. While I believe you and your organization must possess all 5, the gravity and dimension of each is unique. They combine to help you design your singular *trust mosaic*.

Let's get to work.

1. Leadership Vision

"Good business leaders create a vision, articulate the vision, passionately own the vision, and relentlessly drive it to completion."
Jack Welch

Leadership Vision is widely accepted as a critical quality for any senior leader, in particular CEOs. But leadership vision is so much more than that. It is not just for senior leaders; it's for any leader and one of the most powerful trust building weapons in the leadership arsenal. I have debated the "chicken and egg" theory of Vision and Trust with many of my friends. I do not believe the premise that a leader must be trusted first to imbue and energize the organization around their Vision. I subscribe to the belief that it's Leadership Vision that builds the trust in an organization, but also Leadership Vision is a mandate for any person that leads at any level. Whoa! That can't be right. Why not? Only the most senior leaders can have a Vision for their team. I don't believe that. I've had a Vision for every team I have ever led at every level and point of my career. Vision is about clarity and transparency around the strategy, mission, purpose, and values. If you are a leader, you have a need for those for your team, especially if new to a company or a role. This is how you build trust. It's in all of our nature to fear ambiguity, uncertainty, lack of purpose, and lack of destination.

Use your Leadership Vision to combat that fear. Throughout my career, the one constant factor attributed to destroying or preventing trust is fear. It is virtually impossible for fear and trust to co-exist. So, if you want your team, any team at any level, to trust, you must focus on your Leadership Vision.

2. Leadership Character

"Leadership is a potent combination of strategy and character. But if you must be without one, be without the strategy".
Norman Schwarzkopf

When it comes to trusted leadership and building trust, character is probably the most complex, misunderstood, underappreciated, and least written about quality. Yet, it is impossible to be a trusted leader

40

or create a high trust organization without it. Let's talk about one high trust organization. I reference back to the Gallup poll we reviewed earlier. Of the 15 measured institutions, The Military at a 73% trust factor was #1 in the poll and by a respectable 5 percentage point margin over #2. In fact, for the entire span of time Gallup has been taking this measure (May 1973), The Military has been the most trusted institution of them all, on every poll and by a wide margin, reaching all-time highs of 82% in June of 2003 and June of 2009.

The primary mission of the military is to protect and defend the United States and its interests, which can involve engagement in life or death situations. What greater trust can an individual put in their leader than their life or well-being. Trust is everything. The military could not function without trust, and military leadership has always understood that fact. I believe that's why the military has a hyper focus on leadership character. Character is THE most important leadership quality in the military by a long shot. Case in point, let's look at the United States Military Academy at West Point. Acknowledged worldwide as one of, if not the preeminent, school for leadership, it has produced a who's who of recognized great (and trusted) leaders:

- Dwight D. Eisenhower
- Ulysses S. Grant
- Douglas MacArthur
- George S. Patton
- Mike Krzyzewski
- Buzz Aldrin
- Norman Schwarzkopf, Jr
- Stanley A. McChrystal

The list goes on and on and on. I don't think it's an accident that this institution consistently produces highly trusted leaders. It is all about the focus on character.

The mission of West Point:

"To educate, train and inspire the Corps of Cadets so that each graduate is a commissioned leader of <u>character</u> committed to the values of Duty, Honor, Country and prepared for a career of professional excellence and service to the Nation as an officer in the Unites States Army"

The mission statement is clear; the reason West Point exists is to produce a leader of character. Not of great inspiration, strategy, passion, focus, innovation or decisiveness. It's all about character. I don't believe it's an accident or a coincidence that The Military has been the most trusted institution every year for the last three decades. I think this is a direct result of The Military's relentless focus on character. Clearly, I am biased as a West Point graduate, but the West Point mission and my desire to be a leader of character was the primary reason I chose the Academy to further my education over several other premier universities.

While I've found a dozen variations on the definition of character, they all seem to coalesce around a list of virtues and values. The U.S. Army defines 23 mandatory traits of leadership character: Bearing, Confidence, Courage, Integrity, Decisiveness, Justice, Endurance, Tact, Initiative, Coolness, Maturity, Improvement, Will, Assertiveness, Candor, Sense of humor, Competence, Commitment, Creativity, Self-discipline, Humility, Flexibility, Empathy/Compassion.

You are reading that correctly; the U.S. Army has identified a sense of humor as an expected Character trait of its leaders.

To be a trusted leader, focus on the traits of your character; if you want a high trust organization, focus on the character traits of your leaders. Character matters!

3. **Respect and Appreciation**:

"What creates trust, in the end, is the leader's manifest respect for the followers."
Jim O'Toole

"Without appreciation and respect for other people, true leadership becomes ineffective, if not impossible."
George Foreman

Respect and Appreciation are two powerful interconnected and mutually supportive trust building qualities in a leader.

Respect is defined as a feeling of deep admiration for someone or something elicited by their abilities, qualities, or achievements. There is an obvious and concrete connection between respect and trust. In my personal and professional life, I have always respected the leaders I trust and trusted the leaders I respected. The antecedent is also true; I have never respected a leader I did not trust nor trusted a leader I did not respect. You must ask yourself those questions and decide if they ring true for you. If you accept that respect and trust are interconnected, then if we build respect, we build trust. More precisely, as you earn more respect, you will build more trust.

Respect must be earned day in and day out by how you lead and behave. Respect is not given to you just because of title, position, or power. Respect is two-way street – for it to work, it must be mutual. Any leader can earn respect if they will put in the work.

- Maintain your composure, always – Leaders are under a tremendous amount of pressure to deliver results, so when mistakes happen and something goes awry, if you are not careful with your emotions, you can lose respect in a blink of an eye Leaders are respected for always maintaining their composure and being cool under pressure.

  Think about the last time you witnessed a leader lose their composure. Did it shake your confidence in that leader? Did you question that leader's ability to get you through a tough business situation?

  A trusted leader should never lose their composure – publicly or privately.

- Show a strong work ethic – People respect leaders that consistently prove themselves with a strong work

43

ethic. Show you are willing to get your hands dirty and put in the work. Set the tone for the pace, commitment, and passion you want for the organization.

I remember during my first roles at PepsiCo – leadership at one of the distribution facilities in West Virginia. I was fresh out of the military and knew nothing about warehousing, distributing, or selling Pepsi products, but I knew how to lead and how to work. So, I focused on what I knew and committed to learn what I did not. In my first 90 days, I got my hands dirty. Each day, I would be at the facility at 5am to help count inventory and load out the route trucks, then I would ride all day with the route drivers (which gave me a chance to connect with them, meet their customers, stack displays with them, and check out the competition). I learned how to operate a forklift, so I could assist the warehouse team off loading at night. You name it, I did it. The opportunity to learn everything from the ground up was unparalleled. I was the new leader, and I could have easily justified being at my desk pushing paper, but I needed to build trust with the team, so I started by working to earn their respect.

- Admit when you are wrong or if you make a mistake.

- Be punctual – respect your people's time – nothing shows disrespect like showing up late to a town hall, team meeting, or one on one you are leading.

- Be consistent.

Appreciation means to grasp the nature of worth, quality, or significance of. This differs from recognition, which is to acknowledge or notice in some defined way. Anyone can be recognized, and recognition is a good thing for a leader to do, but recognition by itself doesn't earn respect. Now appreciation, authentic and heartfelt appreciation, earns you respect. When people feel appreciated by you, they understand that you have taken the time and made the effort to grasp the nature of their worth, value, quality, and contribution. This investment in them will earn you their respect, and when people observe the appreciation you show to others, it earns you their respect.

4. **Competence and Confidence**:

"Competence is a great creator of confidence."
Mary Jo Putney

"Competence goes beyond words. It's the leader's ability to say it, plan it, and do it in such a way that others know that you know how – and know that they want to follow you."
John C. Maxwell

These two mutually supporting trust building qualities provide a slow to ignite but long-lasting boost and expansion of a leader's trust. The caution is that these two items are complex and delicate. They must be engaged and deployed in the right balance or they could have a negative impact on trust. If a leader's competence quality is out of balance, they may either start to do the work for their team, or worse, because of their knowledge level, micromanage their team, in both cases creating a trust erosion. The leader that is out of balance with the confidence quality could give off the perception of being arrogant, infallible, unapproachable, or even narcissistic. In this scenario, people start to believe the leader cares most about themselves and is willing to do anything to achieve their needs. As a leader, you need to be knowledgeable and self-aware of the risks associated with being out of balance but recognize the sustained results these two qualities contribute to building trust will overshadow all potential risks.

Competence: Being competent is defined as having the ability, knowledge, or skill to do something successfully. The best way to show competence in your role as a leader is to get results. When you deliver results, the team starts to believe in you, building trust that you are the leader that can help them get what they need – a raise, bonus, or new role. You start to believe in you – allowing you to build trust in yourself and your ability to take the right actions and make the right decisions to do your job. Your boss and peers start to believe in you, building trust that you are the right leader for the job, and your peers trust they have the right teammate to help the team achieve their desired results. Competence in results is a powerful trust builder

Confidence: Confidence is defined as having a feeling of self-assurance arising from one's appreciation of one's own abilities and qualities. We have discussed the power of fear and how fear becomes the foundation of mistrust. One of the best weapons a leader can use to combat fear is confidence.

When I first joined the 82nd Airborne Division, I had a morbid fear of heights. I know, you are probably thinking that sounds crazy. Why would you join the Airborne, whose primary mission is to jump out of airplanes, if you were scared to death of being Airborne? Well, maybe it was because I was not that bright in my youth or maybe my truth is that I had spent my whole life face to face with different types of fear, and I learned, once I confronted and pushed back on those fears, I could be the leader and the person I wanted to be... no limits. Did that stop my morbid fear? Nope, not one bit. But it gave me the courage to put on a brave face and suit up with my soldier's every time we had an airborne operation. But it was not pleasant; despite the brave face, inside I was a wreck, shaking, nauseated, and constantly contemplating how many things could go horribly wrong and how many ways I could die. It was a miserable time for me until...

I went to jumpmaster school. Jumpmasters are the expert paratroopers in an airborne unit, responsible for managing airborne jump operations from beginning until they jump out of the airplane. For an airborne operation, each airplane would have a primary jump master(PJM), usually a commissioned officer like myself, and an assistant jumpmaster (AJM), usually a senior noncommissioned officer. In Jumpmaster School, I learned every aspect of an airborne operation. I learned how to rig and inspect parachutes, how to recognize and respond to hazardous situations, how to lean out of the door during flight looking forward to identifying the upcoming drop zone, and looking behind to ensure the trailing aircraft was at a higher altitude than mine. I learned to recognize unsafe movements and equipment issues inside the aircraft and even how to react and respond to fear in the paratroopers that manifested itself as a hesitancy or a refusal to jump out of the aircraft. Most important, I learned the one rule a Jumpmaster would never compromise – DO NOT sacrifice safety for any reason.

46

My airborne knowledge and competency increased **one hundred fold.** I took you through all of that to say this. After Jumpmaster School, I never experienced the old level of morbid fear again for an airborne operation. Sure, I had a healthy dose of normal human concern for doing something as crazy as jumping out of an airplane, but never fear. I counteracted fear with competence and confidence gained from Jumpmaster school. I had a level of knowledge and understanding about all aspects of an Airborne operation I never had before. I understood the skill, knowledge, abilities, and focus on safety of the Jumpmaster that was in charge of the aircraft. I also had a different level of confidence in my ability to recognize and respond to an unsafe situation. My increased competence gave me the confidence to manage my fear. This allowed me to become a better leader. Everyone has fear or concern before an airborne operation. Now that I owned my fear, I could focus on providing a new level of assurance and confidence to my soldiers, easing their fears and earning their trust. As a leader, when you can minimize whatever fear or anxiety your team is feeling, you build trust.

Airborne All the Way!

Assuming you are not getting ready to lead your soldiers on an airborne operation, here are some solid best practices and tactics I have used to build trust through leadership confidence.

- Control how much you talk – confident leaders choose their words carefully and only speak when they have something relevant to say. Babbling is a sign of low confidence.

- Watch your Body Language – ensure you are sending signals of confidence. Stand tall – good posture, use open gestures, lower the pitch and speed of your words, smile, maintain friendly eye contact, and don't fear periods of silence.

- Ask more questions and engage in active listening.

- Express gratitude often.

- Be open to taking risks.

- Learn how to accept compliments – gracefully.

- Never lose your composure.

- Be comfortable in your own skin.

- Learn how to deflect credit to the people on your team – share the spotlight.

- Be willing to stand your ground on your values and beliefs.

Empathy:

"Leadership is about empathy. It is about having the ability to relate to and connect with people for the purpose of inspiring and empowering their lives."
Oprah Winfrey

Empathy is simply the ability to understand and share the feelings of another. It is one of the most powerful qualities to build connections and relationships. Strong connections and relationships with your team builds trust. Empathy is the basis of trust. You probably have heard some variation of "People don't care how much you know until they know how much you care." How about "People don't care about what you want or need until you care about what they want or need"? In whatever case, we are circling around the same point – if a person believes their leader does not know or care about what they want or need, it is highly unlikely they will trust that leader. If they believe a leader would make decisions without consideration of their own personal interests, then they will fear that leader. As we talked about earlier, fear and trust do not mutually coexist. As humans, we're programmed with some innate level of empathy. As a leader, your level of empathy will affect your ability to be trusted. So how do you increase your leadership empathy? Here are a few suggestions:

- **Listening Skills** – If you had to focus on only one skill to help improve your leadership empathy, it would be listening skills. To understand others and connect with what they are feeling, you must be a great listener. Great listening skills mean, not only does the leader really hear what the other person is saying, but the leader is also providing verbal and nonverbal feedback, demonstrating to the person that they are being heard. When a person feels like they are being heard, they feel like they are getting respect, and respect leads to trust. There are very specific active listening skills any leader can learn.

    i. Pay Attention – look at the person directly, cease all distractions, and observe the speaker's body language.

    ii. Show you are listening – ensure you have positioned yourself to listen – full body open and facing the speaker, nod and use facial expressions.

    iii. Provide active listening feedback – paraphrase and repeat back what they are saying, clarify what you are hearing, ask questions, show curiosity.

    iv. Hold Judgement – allow the speaker to finish their thoughts or points without debate or interruptions.

    v. Summarize and respond appropriately – be transparent and candid in your response, treat the other person with respect, even if you don't agree with what they just told you.

- **Emotional Intelligence** – Make a commitment to building emotional intelligence (EQ). EQ is the capacity to be aware of, control, and express one's emotion, and to handle interpersonal relationships judiciously and empathetically. According to Daniel Goleman, an American psychologist who helped popularize EQ, there are five elements to it:

    i. Self-awareness – knowing how you feel and how your feelings or actions affect and interact with the people around you

ii. Self-regulation – this is all about control. The ability to resist making rushed or emotional decisions, verbally attacking others, or compromising your values

iii. Motivation – a deep understanding of what motivates you – in work, play, and life

iv. Empathy – having the ability to put themselves in someone else's situation

v. Social skills – having great communication skills with the ability to manage change and resolve conflicts diplomatically

- Don't interrupt people – Leaders should always "hear their people out". Don't stifle or dismiss their concerns casually. Don't rush to judgement and don't change the subject.

- Address people by name – There literally is no more connecting gesture than someone who remembers and uses your name. I would recommend you also know the name of their spouse, if appropriate.

- Gain insights and expertise on body language – This is important in understanding not only what you are receiving from other people but also what you are sending.

Now that we have covered these five critical components of building trust –

- Leadership Vision
- Leadership Character
- Respect and Appreciation
- Competence and Confidence
- Empathy

I want to close by talking about both the catalyst and glue that encompasses everything we have discussed.

Authentic Leadership.

"Most of us want to be authentic. Yet, we are not who we think we are. We are made up of a rich array of facets and possibilities, many of which we ignore because we label them as "bad". We create a cardboard cutout image of ourselves to look good to others. The discord between who we are and the image we have to live up to slowly kills our aliveness. When we suppress parts of ourselves, it lowers our mojo, sense of fulfillment, leadership effectiveness and impact in the workplace."
Henna Inam

The word authentic has many definitions, but the two I want to focus on for our discussion are – 1) worthy of acceptance or belief as conforming to or based on fact, and 2) true to one's own personality, spirit, or character.

I believe you will be challenged to engage fully and successfully in all the trust building strategies and best practices we have discussed, unless you do so from a foundation of your authentic self. Authentic leadership is simply an approach to leadership that emphasizes building the leader's legitimacy through honest relationships with followers. This leadership style is based on the commitment to building trust and engaging the team with your truthful self.

What does Authentic Leadership look like?

- **Authentic Leaders lead with Character** – They recognize that the best way to build individual and organizational trust is through character. This is less about a leadership style and more about the fundamental traits of character. They use Character as the guiding construct to develop their authentic leadership style. This includes coaching, mentorship, empowering their organization, and making difficult business and people decisions. They have a consistency and predictability when actions, decisions, and responses are generated from within the construct of Character.

"Leadership is the capacity and will to rally men and women to a common purpose and the character which inspires confidence."
Bernard Montgomery, British Field Marshal

- **Authentic Leaders are optimists with a vision** – They lead with both insight and foresight. They let their deep intuitive understanding of people and things (insight) educate, hone, and power their ability to predict what will happen or what is needed in the future(foresight). This is a tremendous asset for the VUCA leader.

"A leader will find it difficult to articulate a coherent vision unless it expresses his core values, his basic identity... one must first embark on a formidable journey of self-discovery in order to create vision with authentic soul."
Mihaly Csikszentmihalyi

- **Authentic Leaders lead with high Emotional Intelligence(EQ)** – They lead from the heart and not just the head. They understand that showing their emotions and vulnerability to their teams makes them human, which promotes connection and builds trust. This doesn't mean the authentic leader compromises their emotional composure. But it creates a bridge or platform for the leader to communicate transparently and directly with empathy. They manage their own range of feelings, so they can remain constructive and not destructive. They create positive learning opportunities from mistakes and setbacks. They possess the ability to demonstrate to their teams they genuinely care, even in the midst of difficult conversations or business situations.

"When you can truly understand how others experience your behavior, without defending or judging, you then have the ability to produce a breakthrough in your leadership and team. Everything starts with your self-awareness. You cannot take charge without taking accountability, and you cannot take accountability without understanding how you avoid it."
Loretta Malandro

- **Authentic leaders lead with Humility** – While authentic leaders usually have very high self-esteem, self-respect, and confidence in their abilities, they lead leveraging humility as a strength. These leaders openly listen to all views, especially those they do not agree with. They treat everyone with respect, no matter what level. They are open and receptive to the input and feedback from all sources. They always ask for a second opinion on important decisions. They prioritize the needs and interests of the organization over their own.

"Humility is not thinking less of yourself, it's thinking of yourself less."
C.S. Lewis

- **Authentic Leaders acknowledge who they are and grow** – Through reflection and introspection, authentic leaders have studied themselves, their life story, and the events and issues that have shaped them. They embrace their true self, their character, and their ethical values. They reveal their true selves to their followers. They understand that being authentic is an unlimited license to grow. They do not subscribe to a rigid view of themselves and their leadership style. They are self-actualized individuals, keenly aware of their strengths, their limitations, and their feelings.

"Be your authentic self. Your authentic self is who you are when you have no fear of judgment, or before the world starts pushing you around and telling you who you're supposed to be. Your fictional self is who you are when you have a social mask on to please everyone else. Give yourself permission to be your authentic self."
Dr. Phil

- **Authentic Leaders lead from the front** – They go first. They are highly visible and refuse to sit on the sidelines or hide in their offices. They lead by example and don't ask others to do what they are unwilling to do themselves. They lead with strength and initiative because it instills confidence and courage, communicating the kind of commitment that earns trust.

"A good leader leads from the front. Don't get stuck in the office. Get out, meet people and listen to their stories."
Sir Richard Branson

- **Authentic Leaders are genuine** – They do not act one way in private and another in public. They don't subscribe to the "fake it till you make it" strategy by pretending to be something they are not. They recognize people will expose leaders who are not genuine, and this exposure will be detrimental to trust. They are not afraid to tell it like it is or to share their true self with others. They speak from the heart, are transparent and willing to articulate their ideas without hidden agendas.

"No one man can, for any considerable time, wear one face to himself, and another for the multitude, without finally getting bewildered as to which is the true one."
Nathaniel Hawthorne

- **Authentic Leaders believe in accountability** - They strive for excellence and not perfection. They refuse to hide from their mistakes out of fear of looking weak. They are willing to publicly own their mistakes and learn from them. They will ask others for help and admit what they don't know. In a VUCA (Volatile, Uncertain, Complex, Ambiguous) world, absolute certainty is scarce and at times even the greatest leaders are unsure. Authentic leaders are honest about that, and they mobilize the entire organization to discover answers and solutions.

"Having authority implies accountability. If you reject the blame for failures under your watch, people reject your leadership."
Rick Warren

- **Authentic Leaders are self-aware** – They examine and understand what causes them to behave in certain ways and the impact and influence that behavior has on the people around them. They are well-versed in how their behavioral traits show up differently in response to environmental triggers and stressors.

54

"Self-awareness involves deep personal honesty. It comes from asking and answering hard questions."
Stephen Covey

- **Authentic Leaders are mission driven** – They understand the direct link between getting results and building trust. They lead in pursuit of results, not for their own power, money, or ego. They understand the real measure of their leadership is the impact they have on their team and organization. They believe their job is to make a difference and be instrumental in creating long-term, sustainable value for all stakeholders. They want to leave a legacy of inspiration, innovation, character, respect, and impact that resonates long after they are gone.

"Authenticity is the alignment of head, mouth, heart, and feet – thinking, saying, feeling, and doing the same thing – consistently. This builds trust, and followers love leaders they can trust."
Lance Secretan

There is a widely held view, including me, that believes Authentic Leadership is the "gold standard" for successful leadership. I believe in the VUCA world in which we lead today, that only a trusted leader in a high trust organization will be strategically and tactically prepared to succeed. I've concluded that Authentic Leadership is the best-suited of all leadership styles to face, engage, and counteract the rising wave of distrust that leaders face today. I hope you will join me on the never-ending but fulfilling journey in Building Trust through Authentic Leadership. Welcome aboard!

"For those of you who really want to give critical thought to your unique leadership style and foster genuine followership, learn from what's out there and weave it into something meaningful and authentic."
Stacy Feiner

Build Trust by Leading with Authenticity
Chapter Recap

- Trust is the glue that holds all relationships together – especially the relationship between leader and follower.
- There is a trust crisis in our society today. Leaders are challenged to build trust in a low trust world.
- High trust in an organization is a dividend, while low trust is a tax.
- High trust leaders are required to build high trust organizations.
- Recognize and understand the danger signs of low trust in your organization.
- Adopt and Implement the 5 powerful trust building Strategies.
    - Leadership Vision
    - Leadership Character
    - Respect and Appreciation
    - Competence and Confidence
    - Empathy
- Build Empathy by increasing listening skills and Emotional Intelligence (EQ).
- Build, develop, and nurture your unique Authentic Leadership style.

Parker Principle #3

Courageous Leadership:
Dare to Dream and Dare to Fail

This is my all-time favorite Parker Principle. It contains three of the most important traits associated with Take The Limits Off leadership – Courage, Dreaming, and Failure. These three characteristics are intimately interconnected and when deployed together create a powerful motivational and trust building leadership triad. These three characteristics are all about the heart – a brave heart, a visionary heart, and a heart of perseverance. Let's start with a conversation about courage. Only within the construct of courage can the true positive power of dreaming and failing be emancipated.

"Courage is rightly esteemed as the first of human qualities . . . because it is the quality which guarantees all others."
Winston Churchill, British Prime Minister

As a learning leader, we can find an infinite number of information sources that advocate dozens of "must have" leadership traits, qualities, and virtues. This can be both confusing and overwhelming to any leader trying to build and define their authentic leadership style. This also makes it difficult for a leader to answer critical questions; What are the most compelling and powerful leadership qualities? Of these, which ones should I focus my time, energy and resources to master? Actually, there is no one right answer. To be authentic, there is only your answer. While your leader mosaic will be a "you" original, there is one "must have" characteristic or virtue required in any successful leadership mosaic - Courage. Courage is the one characteristic that will define, solidify, and amplify all others.

Leadership qualities such as innovation, integrity, optimism, responsibility, commitment, confidence, and decision-making are made authentic, compelling, and effective only through the portal of courage.

The truth about courage:

- First, we are each born with some level of innate courage.
- Second, courage is a skill that can be built and strengthened by any leader with the slightest aptitude to be courageous.
- Third, courage is built one moment, one decision, and one action at a time.

In the previous chapter, I talked about my morbid fear of heights and how an increase in my airborne competence helped me to build confidence to help combat that fear. To be candid, the fear never went away. I just refused to be immobilized by it. On every operation, my first jump to my last jump, I had fear. It's just not a natural human concept to voluntarily throw yourself out of an airplane into the blackness of the night sky with only a piece of nylon on your back, praying you do not die when the law of gravity is in place to ensure your prompt return to the earth. I can tell you there is not a single jump in which I called myself brave or courageous, but I understood that my soldiers were watching my every move. As the leader, they expected me to stand up and jump out of the airplane without hesitation or reservation. I had a duty, responsibility, and commitment to my soldiers, so I had to push through the fear and lead. It was not until much later in life, and long after I left the military, that I understood that every time I suited up, put on a brave face, and launched myself into the sky, it was an act of courage. Only then did I comprehend that it got a tiny bit easier to push through that fear on each subsequent jump. This resulted in me building courage. Each act of courage built more courage.

> *"I learned that courage was not the absence of fear, but the triumph over it. The brave man is not he who does not feel afraid, but he who conquers that fear."*
> **Nelson Mandela**

Courage (and cowardice) are organizationally infectious characteristics. A courageous leader nurtures and inspires courage within their teams and organization. A courageous organization will perform better in the marketplace, especially in a **V.U.C.A.** world. They will face **Volatility** without fear. They will not be paralyzed or incapacitated by **Uncertainty**. They will innovate in the midst of **Complexity**. They will trust in their abilities and intuition when confronted with **Ambiguity**. A courageous organization can push past any artificial limits and achieve unparalleled success. I recommend you take a moment of reflection and ask yourself two questions:

- Am I a courageous leader?
- Do I work in a courageous organization?

If your answer is yes to both questions, then congratulations, you are in the top 5% of all organizations.

If you are in that top 5% then you have/are:

- Over-achieved your annual operating plan for two or more consecutive years.
- Maximized your personal and team pay raises and bonuses.
- Achieved Marketplace leadership.
- Experienced great success at recruiting, developing, and retaining the top talent in your industry.

The list can go on and on. Once again, my sincere congratulations, you are living the life that the other 95% of us aspire to live. If you are with me and a part of the other 95%, let's talk about some actionable processes and best practices you can start today to be the courageous leader your team deserves and build the courageous organization that your team needs.

"Courage is more exhilarating than fear and in the long run it is easier. We do not have to become heroes overnight. Just a step at a time, meeting each thing that comes up, seeing it is not as dreadful as it appeared, discovering we have the strength to stare it down."
Eleanor Roosevelt

Ranger School:

Ranger School is one of the toughest training courses in the Army. The stated purpose of the U.S. Army's Ranger Course is to prepare these Army leaders in combat arms related functional skills with the primary mission to engage in close combat and direct-fire battles. Army Rangers are experts in leading soldiers on difficult missions— and to do this, they need rigorous training. Ranger students train to mental and physical exhaustion, pushing past any pre-existing limits of their

59

minds and bodies. Soldiers enrolled in this combat leadership course must endure great mental and psychological stresses while coping with the physical fatigue of combat. What should a Ranger student expect?

- Over two months (72 days when I attended) of 20 hour days of physical and mental exertion
- To carry between 65-90 lbs. of combat equipment
- Tactical foot movements of 200+ miles
- One or fewer meals each day with 0 to 5 hours of sleep a night
- 6 or more graded leadership positions with Peer evaluations after each phase
- Three intense training phases – Benning, Mountain, and Swamp (4 phases when I went –Desert)
- 3 to 4 Airborne Operations
- Pass a Combat Water Survival Assessment
- Pass a Land Navigation Assessment
- A Graduation Rate between 30% and 40% of attendees

For any normal human, the list above would create enough apprehension and anxiety to erase any desire to attend. In addition, before you can even consider the whether you are insane enough to attend Ranger School, you must get a slot in a class. That is a monumental task.

Ranger School is open to all qualified soldiers in the U.S. Army… if you can get a slot, or more appropriately, earn a slot. I was in the 82nd Airborne Division, and earning a slot to Ranger School is a lot like buying a winning lottery ticket. The odds are stacked against you. To earn a slot to Ranger School from the 82nd, you must overcome three Major obstacles:

1. Slot Availability: The chart below provides the statistical data of the # of attendees and graduation rates by unit for Ranger School in 2016. Note that the 82nd Airborne Division received just under **7%** (267) of all available slots (4009) for 2016.

Unit	Grad Rate	Total Attendees
1st Armored Division	22.9%	35
1st Cavalry Division	37.5%	16
1st Infantry Division	33.3%	30
10th Mountain Division	34.2%	202
101st Airborne Division	28.5%	172
2nd Infantry Division	26.2%	42
25th Infantry Division	30.7%	244
3rd Infantry Division	21.3%	108
4th Infantry Divison	28.2%	39
7 ID/ I Corps	27.3%	22
75th Ranger Regiment	56.7%	554
82nd Airborne Division	37.8%	267
173rd	20.7%	140
ABOLC	21.9%	178
IBOLC	40.6%	936
International Students	32.4%	71
MCCC	16.5%	85
National Guard	43.8%	89
Other BOLC	32.5%	80
Other CCC	11.1%	18
Sister Services	42.9%	28
USAOC	49.8%	203
Other Units	28.4%	450

(2) Units with mandatory pre-Ranger courses (PRC) such as the 75th Ranger Regiment, National Guard, and 82nd Airborne Division, tne to have higher graduation rates than other units.

(3) The top sources (those units that send the most Students) include: Infantry Basic Officer Leadership Course (IBOLC), 75th Ranger Regiment, 82nd Airborne Division, 25th Infantry Division, and United States Army Special Operations Command (USASOC).

2. Mandatory Pre-Ranger course: The chart above also shows the graduation rate for each unit, which is also a badge of pride for the unit. When you look at the high attendee sources (5%> of slot allocation): The 82nd Airborne Division is #3 behind the Infantry Basic Officer Leadership Course (IBOLC) and the 75th Ranger Regiment. In addition, of the 13 listed regular U.S. Army units, the 82nd Airborne Division is #2 in graduation rate at 37.8% behind the 75th Ranger Regiment at 56.7%. The 82nd's above average graduation rate is not by accident. Just look at the bottom of the chart above and note (2) *Units with **mandatory** pre Ranger courses such as...82nd Airborne Division have higher graduation rates than other units.* The 82nd Pre-Ranger Course (PRC) is an intense and rigorous 17-day course that provides a curriculum and training that mirrors

the mental and physical stress and challenges of the first two weeks of Ranger School. PRC has a failure rate of almost 60%. This mandatory course was put in place to provide an intense screening process, so graduates that eventually earn a slot will have the best possible chance of successfully graduating from Ranger School. It specifically mirrors the first two weeks of Ranger School because, historically, those first two weeks, RAP (Ranger Assessment Program) weeks, account for the vast majority of Ranger School failures. For 2016, of the 63.2% of the candidates that failed Ranger School, 44.3% failed during the RAP weeks.

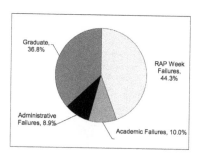

3. The Competition: I chose to serve in the 82nd Airborne Division as my first duty assignment specifically because it was widely accepted that serving in the 82nd Airborne Division would be one of the toughest duty assignments you could choose coming out of West Point or any school as a newly commissioned Officer. For me, this was the dream assignment – the 82nd, where the most talented leaders go to test their ability to lead. The 82nd's mission is "to within 18 hours of notification, strategically deploy, conduct a forcible entry parachute assault and secure key objectives for follow-on military operations in support of U.S. national interests." That mission requires the 82nd to have intense day to day training to maintain the highest state of readiness well above the levels of other Army divisions. Expectations on leaders in the 82nd are extremely high, with no tolerance for leaders that do not excel.

Let me summarize; just to earn a slot to Ranger School, I would have to 1) compete with the best leaders in the elite 82nd Airborne Division just for a chance to attend the Pre-Ranger Course. 2) Subject myself to 17 grueling days of hell in the Pre-Ranger Course – with a 60% chance that I would fail. 3) Even If I beat the odds and graduated from the Pre ranger Course(PRC), I would have to compete against the other PRC graduates to get one of the 7% allocation of 82nd Airborne slots. All the above, just to have the opportunity to attend a school for over 70 days with a +30% chance of graduation. You're right; that is just good old fashioned crazy.

"You gain strength, courage, and confidence by every experience in which you really stop to look fear in the face. You must do the thing which you think you cannot do."
Eleanor Roosevelt

So why did I go? I didn't need Ranger School. I was an Artillery Officer. Ranger School is most relevant to the skillset and leadership requirements of Infantry Officers. Career wise, life was perfect. I was in a great unit, my team was absolutely outstanding, and I had gotten a rare and glorious #1 block on my first Officer Evaluation Report. The stars were aligned, and everything was going my way. So why did I go? Why would I risk embarking on a mission that could end in cataclysmic failure? A journey that had from 10 to 20 failure waypoints and failing any one of them meant failure of the total mission, which was graduating from Ranger School. So why risk so much for something I did not need? It was actually simple and not that crazy. Ranger School represented the culmination of all my worst and most debilitating fears.

Fear of Failure – This was probably the most significant of all the fears. I was a farm boy that, against all odds, made it off the farm, graduated from West Point, and was leading with great success in the 82nd Airborne Division. While my self-esteem was high and I had great confidence in my leadership, mental, and physical abilities…what if? What if I could not get into the Pre-Ranger Course(PRC)? What if I failed PRC? What if I passed PRC and could not get a Ranger School slot? What if I failed Ranger School? I had failed at little in my life and this could be the first domino to fall, leading to a lifetime of future failures.

Fear of Leadership Ineptitude – I viewed leadership as my craft, and I was a devoted student of that craft. I read and incorporated every good leadership process and principle that made sense and fit my leadership style. But…what if all that falls apart when my leadership is tested under extreme mental and physical conditions? I thought of myself as a humble "leader of the people," but I was an officer. I was by rank and assignment put in charge of my soldiers. They did not choose me. I just showed up and took over. I knew that, in Ranger School, you had to remove all rank insignia; everyone was equal and you had to lead through credibility alone. What if could not do that? What if I was more reliant on positional authority than I let myself believe? What if my fellow Ranger candidates would not follow me? What if my leadership style caused me to be hated by my Ranger candidate peers? A rarely talked about part of Ranger School is the peer evaluations. They happen at the end of each phase, and if you get rated low by your peers? You guessed it! You Fail the school and get sent home.

Fear of Physical Inadequacy: I have always considered myself physically and mentally strong. A good athlete but not great. Could I physically handle the requirements of Ranger School? Over 200 miles on foot, carrying as much as 90lbs, with the 1 meal a day hunger pains, and 0 to 5 hours of sleep a night for 72 days? While I thought I was a physical "stud", I knew in my heart I had never been tested with such extremes. What if I could not handle it or got hurt? Yep... I fail the school and get sent home.

Fear of Being a Weak Swimmer: I could swim a little, but I was not a strong swimmer. What if I failed the Ranger Combat Water Survival Assessment (CWSA)? Just to give you perspective, the CWSA consists of three mandatory events:

- **Log Walk Rope Drop:** The Ranger student will climb a 35ft tower, walk 70ft across a log suspended 35ft in the air, ascend three steps, climb from the log onto a rope suspended 35 feet in the air then commando crawl along the rope to the center of a lake and drop 35 feet into the water. Swim to shore while wearing your ACU's (Army Combat Uniform) and combat boots.
- **Slide for Life:** The ranger student will climb a 75ft tower, slide 150 meters down a cable, drop into the middle of a lake then swim to shore while wearing ACU's and combat boots.
- **Equipment Removal and 15 Meter Swim:** The Ranger student will jump into a pond with full combat gear and rifle then successfully discard their gear while staying submerged.

If any part of the students' body or equipment comes out of the water...Fail. Once you discard all equipment then the Ranger student must swim 15 meters while wearing ACU's and combat boots then exit the pond.

Fail any of the three events, you fail the CSWA. Fail the CSWA, you fail the Ranger course and...Yep! Get sent home! If that was not bad enough add the fact that you must execute all three events with NO hesitation or any other outward sign of fear. You show fear, you fail the CSWA, and you got the rhythm... get sent home.

Fear of Being Lost: Land navigation is a core competency in Ranger School. The Day/Night Land Timed Navigation test is the Ranger student boogey man. It is the biggest failure event (11% of all students) outside of RAP week. While I don't consider myself directionally challenged, how many of us have been caught out in the middle of the woods, in the dark of night, with just a compass and a map to find your way to half a dozen check points, miles and miles apart from each other? Oh, by the way, you cannot use your flashlight to navigate only to grab the occasional quick snapshot view of your map. What if I can't navigate? What if I need to use my flashlight? What if I have a poor sense of direction or poor ability to understand terrain? What if I can't find all the checkpoints within the required time? Miss any of the above, you fail land navigation. You fail land navigation, you fail Ranger School. Even if you pass the land navigation test, you must be in the leader position on at least six missions during the three phases. As the leader of a mission, you may have to take your team 10 or more miles through the mountains, swamp, or desert to the objective. If you get lost along the way, you fail that mission. You fail 3 or more missions, you fail Ranger School.

Fear of Fear: I recognized that I had a morbid fear of heights. What if I couldn't handle the 3 or 4 Airborne Operations in Ranger School? This was before I went to jumpmaster school, built my courage, and developed my Airborne Zen. What if I couldn't find the courage to climb mountains or rappel off cliffs during the Mountain Phase? Then there is the famous swamp phase, where you can spend days walking through swamps in water up to or above your chest. Guess what swamps have? A lot of snakes and a fair share of alligators. You guessed it. I have a little bit of a problem with reptiles. What if I could not push through and conquer my fears? Failure.

Fear of Mental Fragility – Was I mentally tough and resilient enough to face: all my fears, physical exhaustion, mental duress, sleep deprivation and not quit. I had no idea how I would react with so many fears and challenges all coming to bear at one time. I would need to face, manage, and conquer not one of them but all of them. We talked about all the elite competition, preparation, and training it takes to get to Ranger School. Even with that, each year, between 2% and 4% of Ranger students fail due to Lack of Motivation (LOM). Meaning, at some point in the course, they just cannot take another step or another day and they quit. If you have seen the movie G.I. Jane, in which Demi Moore plays an Officer and the first female to attend Navy SEAL School, they have a bell in the middle of the courtyard, and if you want to quit, you make the slow emotional walk to the bell and ring it - LOM. Now Ranger school doesn't have anything that dramatic; you just whisper to a Ranger Instructor that you quit and "poof" you magically disappear never to be seen again. The funny thing about Ranger School, you can fail and get sent home in almost any other manner and you get to come back and try again. If you LOM – you can never return. What if I break? What if one of my fears gets the best of me? I did not believe I was capable of quitting, but I had never been pushed to the extreme limitations that Ranger School would push me. Ranger School will make me find and face my true-self. What if I did not like what I found – no bravery, no courage just bluster? What if?

> *"Everything you've ever wanted is on the other side of fear."*
> **George Addair**

Ranger School was the embodiment of almost everything I feared. It was my black hole. I could either face it and be a survivor or face it and be defeated. I just had to muster up enough courage to face it.

Ranger School changed my life forever. I had to face so many fears and build just enough courage to overcome them, time after time, one by one. What I didn't notice until after graduation was that every action and decision in the face of fear added a brick to my Courage Citadel.

A Citadel is a fortress used in defense during an attack or siege. My Courage Citadel is the fortress I use to protect my courage when I am attacked by fears. Every attack makes my citadel bigger and stronger.

By the time I graduated and earned my Ranger Tab, my Courage Citadel was strong, secure, and impenetrable. I relished facing fears, taking the power from them, and making it my own. It became a badge of honor, and I have endeavored to live each day with a little more courage and a little less fear than the day before. I think we all have fears that affect us. But today, we will be courageous. We will commit to taking the appropriate actions right now to build courage in ourselves and in our organization.

Let's talk about ways to build greater and greater courage.

Face your Fears and Take Action- What is the source of our courage? Are we born with courage? Of course, we are. I subscribe to the belief that all people are born with some measure of courage. While there are varying amounts of innate courage in each individual, we all have a courage baseline. Our courage either builds or recedes from that baseline with every action taken or decision made. Facing a fear is a direct way to build courage and add to your baseline. Each time we stand up to fear, we build courage. No matter what the outcome, the simple act of facing fear builds courage. With age comes wisdom, and when I look back at the decision to jump into the Ranger School black hole, I still held the belief that, if I failed to graduate, my courage baseline would be negatively affected. I understand today that was an incorrect assumption. The simple act of facing the fears associated with Ranger School built courage. Every Airborne operation- cliff rappel, water test, land navigation test, ranger patrol...every fear faced built more courage, regardless of whether I graduated Ranger School.

Here is an exercise:

Take a moment and list your top ten fears - Five Leadership Fears and Five Personal Fears. Write them down. With a little honest self-reflection, this exercise should be easy. At some point in time in my career, I've had to deal with quite a few leadership fears; maybe you will find your five in my list:

- Criticism
- Public Speaking
- Being an unpopular leader
- Uncertainty - Not being able to predict and prepare for the future business environment

- Failure
- Rejection
- Making bad decisions
- Leadership competence
- Not having enough emotional intelligence

"Nothing in life is to be feared, it is only to be understood. Now is the time to understand more, so that we may fear less."
Marie Curie

You may be thinking, wow that's a long list. I agree, but it's real. I acknowledge, recognize, and accept these as my fears and spend much of my time engaging in best practices to conquer them.

- **Awareness and Identification** – before you can overcome a fear, you must be aware of it. If you have behaviors that seem to be negatively affecting your career or your relationships, there is probably a fear at its source. Identify your fears.

- **Understanding** – Once identified, it is important that you try to understand the source of your fear – falling out of a tree as a child, almost drowning…

- **Engagement Plan** – Develop a plan to engage your fears at every opportunity. This is how you build courage. The optimum plan allows you to face off with one of your fears frequently. Put together a plan to engage each of your five business fears at least four times a month. Each time you engage that fear, you will gain experience and courage

- **Taking Action to Erase Negative Thoughts** – Get smart. Acquire all the knowledge you can about your fear, then go face it. It is important that, when you face that fear, you leverage your new knowledge to generate optimism. Rewire your brain and think positive thoughts in the face of your fear.

- **Practice, practice, practice** – It doesn't matter what your fears are; if you practice, you will conquer. If you fear swimming, swim regularly. If you fear public speaking, speak in public as often as you can. You will get better, less fearful, and more courageous after each one.

- **Talk and Write** – If you have a trusted source (friend, mentor, pastor, priest…) talk about your fear with them. It will actually empower you and give you confidence when you can comfortably talk about your fear. Keep a journal. Make an entry when you engage in a fear driven negative behavior. Understand your triggers and responses.

"The thing you fear most has no power. Your fear of it is what has the power. Facing the truth really will set you free."
Oprah Winfrey

Here are a few other best practices to combat fear or build courage that have proved effective throughout my life:

- **Face the Truth, Confront Reality and Act**

- **Lead Change**

- **Reward Failure**

- **Act Decisively**

- **Challenge Your Comfort Zone**

- **Insure a Culture of Dignity and Respect**

- **Set High Moral and Ethical Standards**

- **Speak Plainly**

- **Seek 360-degree feedback, acknowledge, absorb and act**

- **Lead with High Visibility**

- **Give Credit to Others**

This wasn't meant to be an all-inclusive list of best practices; it's simply what has worked for me. Apply the ones that resonate with your authentic self and character. I keep this list as one page in my journal, periodically pulling it out to validate that I am "walking the talk" and doing the things that combat fear and build courage. I put a special level of focus around any areas I find underdeveloped. I hope you will find them useful and actionable.

> *"The encouraging thing is that every time you meet a situation, though you may think at the time it is an impossibility and you go through the tortures of the damned, once you have met it and lived through it you find that forever after you are freer than you ever were before. If you can live through that you can live through anything. You gain strength, courage, and confidence by every experience in which you stop to look fear in the face. You are able to say to yourself, `I lived through this horror. I can take the next thing that comes along.' The danger lies in refusing to face the fear, in not daring to come to grips with it. If you fail anywhere along the line, it will take away your confidence. You must make yourself succeed every time. You must do the thing you think you cannot do."*
> **Eleanor Roosevelt**

Dreams and Failures

Now that we have established the foundational principle of courage, we can talk about Dreams and Failures. Only when planted in the fertile soil of courage can the positive seeds of inspirational dreams and courageous failure thrive and grow. They each, in their own unique way, allow a leader to directly access and engage the singular power and resilience of their soul. This access allows the leader to achieve the impossible and survive the incomprehensible, to push themselves past artificial limits they may have imposed upon their lives.

Dreams

> *"The future belongs to those who believe in the beauty of their dreams."*
> **Eleanor Roosevelt**

At first glance, dreams seem like a soft subject to be a part of a leadership book. But that is only at first glance. There is leadership power not only in dreaming but also in inspiring your people and your organization to share your dream. There are multiple definitions of dreams and they all are relevant to pursuing great leadership and success:

- Thoughts, images, or emotions during sleep
- An experience of waking life having characteristics of a dream, such as a vision or a creation of the imagination
- A state of mind marked by abstraction or release from reality
- Something notable for its beauty, excellence, or enjoyable quality
- Strongly desired goal or purpose

All these are relevant and real in terms of leadership. It is a fact that some of the most notable advancements in mankind result directly from an individual's actual sleep induced dream:

- **Downloading World Wide Web-** The foundational idea for Google came from dreams. Larry Page, Founder of Google, dreamed: "What if we could download the whole web...?" When he woke up, he wrote down his dream and the idea of downloading the web. He shared this idea with co-founder of Google, Sergey Brin.

- **DNA's double helix-** The discovery of DNA's structure is one of the greatest discoveries of all time. James Watson, co-discoverer of the structure of DNA, reportedly dreamed of two snakes intertwined with heads at the opposite ends. It led him to consider the structure as a double helix.

- **The Terminator-**Director James Cameron, with a soaring fever spiking, had a vivid dream, more like a nightmare, which inspired him for the Terminator. He saw a metallic gleaming figure with a rictus smile and piercing burning red eyes, pulling itself up from the fire and dragging across the floor with kitchen knives.

- **Theory of Relativity-** Albert Einstein saw in a dream he was sledding down a mountain in an ever-increasing speed until he noticed the stars looked different because of his speed. From this dream, he realized that things appear differently to different people, depending on the place they are standing and due to the time it takes for light to reach them.

While those are real dreams that had dramatic impact and influence on the world in which we live today, the dreams I want to discuss are more powerful, expansive, compelling, and enduring. Dreams that ignite and inspire the human spirit.

If you doubt the power of dreams, think about the insane success of the lotteries in the United States. The whole concept is powered by dreams. With almost no chance of winning, in 2014, Americans spent almost $70 Billion on legal lotteries in 43 states. Just to break that math down, that is about $300 spent by each adult in those states. The numbers suggest more than half the population plays the lottery. How much did you spend on lottery tickets in the last 12 months? Be honest; it is just you and me here. If you bought a lottery ticket, you are a dreamer. You were willing to invest the time, energy, and money to get to a version of reality you imagined. A world that looks entirely different than the one you live in today, but real and reachable if just....

I am also a part of the lottery dream crowd, so own it.

The same principle applies to Las Vegas, which is basically an entire city powered by and built around dreams. In 2016, Las Vegas had 42.9 million visitors. That is a monumental testament to the power of dreams to "move" people, literally. Most people are familiar with the Las Vegas saying, "The House Always Wins!", meaning if you gamble in Las Vegas, you are likely to leave the city with less money than when you arrived. Clearly, that warning did not stop 43 million people from making the trek.

I have tremendous respect and appreciation for the power of dreams. Now imagine unleashing that power within yourself and within your organization. Imagine the level of success you can achieve in your life and career when you tap into the power of dreams.

72

As a business leader we imbed our dreams within the laws of business: economics, talent, technology, resources... and we call it Vision. One of our intrinsic duties as a leader is to garner our people's buy-in and belief in the Vision. The more imaginative the Dream, the more manifest the Vision, the more substantial the rewards.

"Every great dream begins with a dreamer. Always remember, you have within you the strength, patience and the passion to reach for the stars, to change the world. "
Harriet Tubman

A good leader will live and model the life they seek to inspire in their people! So, every day I try to be a real-life example of why all of us should dream more. Be audacious and unrelenting in your dreams. Reach for the impossible and strive every day to achieve more than you ever thought possible. Dreams should be ridiculous in size! You must truly believe that nothing is out of the realm of possibility and that anything is possible if only you work hard to learn and locate the right path to success.

If you have heard me speak, you know I spent my early years on a farm in rural North Carolina, affectionately known as "the country," where you were as likely to be driving on a dirt road as you were a paved one. Back then, my dream was simply to make it off the farm and get an education. Most of the time, this seemed like an impossible dream. I didn't believe there were a lot of higher education opportunities for a poor black southern "country boy." I understood fully the limits of my reality, but I also had a grandmother who taught me that, while I must acknowledge and respect my reality, I need not accept it. That I should pursue my dreams and strive to live a life without limitations.

"So many of our dreams at first seem impossible, then they seem improbable, and then, when we summon the will, they soon become inevitable."
Christopher Reeve

I not only decided I would pursue my dreams, but I decided to dream bigger, not just dream of doing the remarkable, but dream of doing the ridiculous. Suddenly, it wasn't good enough just to go to college, I wanted to go to West Point. After I graduated from the Academy, it would have been easy to say mission accomplished and put it in cruise control. But it's a funny thing about dreams; when you make one come true, it creates euphoria, a sense of intense happiness and self–confidence, and it lasts... for a little while. Suddenly, there is a yearning that turns into a hunger to dream and strive again, to give yourself the opportunity to feel the euphoria again. That became the mobilizing rhythm of my life.

After West Point, I immediately challenged myself with bigger dreams. Whether it was serving in the 82nd Airborne Division or attending Airborne School, Ranger School, and Jumpmaster School, each of these dreams went through what I use as my big dream life cycle – **Impossible, Improbable then Inevitable**.

When deciding on whether to stay in the military for the 20-year career or pursue a career in the civilian world, I had no empirical evidence I would be able to translate a great military career to corporate success – but I had big dreams and those dreams were bigger than the risk of failure. While I was tenacious and relentless in my pursuit of those dreams, I received a significant amount of pushback from... almost everyone.

As I shared earlier, my military career was progressing way beyond my highest expectations. I attended the greatest Army training schools, my team achieved a successful rotation to the National Training Center, my team performed flawlessly in combat (Desert Storm/Desert Shield), and I returned with my entire team safely home. I received a top performance rating and #1 or #2 block on all my Officer Evaluation Reports. My career progression couldn't have been better. The only

74

problem… I had dreams. Dreams of having a successful career in the corporate world. I didn't even understand what the C-suite was back then, but I knew enough to make that my ridiculous dream. There was resistance to the idea of me leaving the military from almost everyone, including family, peers, senior officers, mentors, and yes, even my grandmother. I understood the dream was mine to own and that if I failed to pursue it, I would be the only one to blame. So, I left the military, without a civilian job in sight, and probably without even a very good plan. But I was excited with it all because I had not compromised or betrayed my dreams.

"If you limit your choices only to what seems possible or reasonable, you disconnect yourself from what you truly want, and all that is left is a compromise."
Robert Fritz

I want to pause to make a very important point. If you want to pursue your dreams, you must make sacrifices, be without a safety net, and even go against the advice of the people you love and respect the most. You must trust yourself, and your inner voice must be the loudest voice in the crowd.

"Don't let the noise of others' opinions drown out your own inner voice."
Bill George

A couple of decades ago, when I started my corporate career, I couldn't have imagined being blessed with the career I have enjoyed. The fact that a young man coming from such humble beginnings could one day have the privilege of being Vice President and General Manager of a multi-billion-dollar technology business unit at Dell and President of Brink's North America, a billion-dollar business unit with over 12,000 team members seems a little ridiculous. Right?

"I tell people I'm too stupid to know what's impossible. I have ridiculously large dreams, and half the time they come true."
Debi Thomas

Failure:

"Only those who dare to fail greatly can ever achieve greatly".
Robert F. Kennedy

I would be remiss if I didn't talk about the most significant impediment to leaders pursuing their dreams, failure. Failure is fickle; it can be friend or foe. It can augment or diminish a dream, build or destroy courage, heighten or hurt trust, even propel or end a career. No matter how strong a leader may be, they will fail. We are human and imperfect creatures, and I will bet you have experienced some level or type of failure in your life. I've experienced more than I would care talk about. If you have never experienced failure, don't feel left out of the club; just live long enough and you will. It's inevitable.

However, how that failure will affect you is not pre-ordained.

How you handle any failure will determine whether it is an ally or an adversary. We can never have enough allies, so what do we do?

"There is only one thing that makes a dream impossible to achieve: the fear of failure."
Paulo Coelho

Earlier, I indicated that dreams must be planted in the fertile soil of courage to grow strong and mighty. The same is true for the version of failure that is our friend and ally. It must be planted in courage. The simple truth is that it takes courage to dare to fail and courage to recover from failure. Don't let the possibility or even the probability of failure intimidate you. It's OK to fail. Here are some ways to make failure your friend:

"Take chances, make mistakes. That's how you grow. Pain nourishes your courage. You have to fail in order to practice being brave."
Mary Tyler Moore

1. **Failure is the greatest mechanism for learning ever developed in the history of the world.** – I have significant confidence in that statement. If you can think of a better learning tool...let me know. Every great invention and advancement in the history of mankind has come on the heels

of failure, often multiple failures. Just think about some of the momentous positive results from failure. Some famous failures: Alexander Fleming(Penicillin), Spencer Silver (Post-It Notes), Charles Goodyear (Vulcanization, Plastic), Constatin Fahlberg (Saccharine) and Wilson Greatbach (The Pacemaker).

Two of our most famous inventors, Thomas Edison (Light Bulb, Phonograph) and Benjamin Franklin (Kite, Bifocals), were also proud serial failures – Edison (Electric Pen, Talking Doll), Franklin (Hair Based Liquor, Crotchless Beekeeping Suit). The wonderful irony about failure is it teaches the leader about the "weight and impact" of their decisions, innovation, risk mitigation, business continuity, and resilience.

In Parker Principle #1 – Leadership is Learning, I introduced you to the AAR (After Action Review) for the organization. As a reminder, the AAR is simply a highly structured process to help provide the program, project, or event team feedback on the mission and task performances. While this is a great organizational learning tool, especially in the face of a failure, it is also a great individual leader learning tool. Throughout my career, I've also used a "Mel" version to evaluate all my big decisions, successes, and failures. While modified for my individual leadership review, I basically maintained the same construct. The Leader AAR process consists of the same four parts:

a. `**Planning the AAR** – I put a formal event on my calendar, minimum an hour in length, sometimes two, depending upon the complexity and magnitude of the decision.

b. **Preparing for the AAR** – I gather all relevant decision information to include feedback from all affected people, usually a simple survey done with survey monkey, and I try to keep it less than 10 survey questions (1 thru 10 rating) and 3 to 4 open ended commentary questions. You will be surprised what you learn. Little things that wouldn't even register as significant to the leader can come back as major misses. This is especially important when your decision affects multiple countries – account for cultural, language, and even holiday differences.

c. **Conduct the AAR** – Conduct an honest analysis of all data and feedback and answer the 4 basic questions:

o What was expected to happen?
o What actually happened? What went well and why?
o What can be improved?
o How can it be improved?
o **AAR Follow Up** – Discuss and Brief your findings, first with your boss, then with your team, then with the entire organization. Share your learnings, honestly own your mistakes, and lay out the actions to be taken to ensure what went well is repeated and what went wrong is corrected.

"Failure should be our teacher, not our undertaker. Failure is delay, not defeat. It is a temporary detour, not a dead end. Failure is something we can avoid only by saying nothing, doing nothing, and being nothing."
Denis Waitley

I guarantee this process will help you turn a negative failure into a positive learning event. You will build credibility and trust with your team, and it will make you a better leader.

2. **Trust Your Instinct, Make a Decision, and Act Quickly** – Under all circumstances, avoid failure paralysis. It is a career limiter for any leader, especially senior leaders. You make a decision, things go sideways, failure happens then you go dark. You must not hide from the effects of your decision, your team, or making another decision. The absolute worse action you can take after a failure is no action. It just compounds the failure, and it erodes your team's confidence and trust in your leadership. I am not a horse person but "when you fall off a horse, you should immediately get back on" rings true here. The longer you wait to make a big decision after a bad decision, the harder it will become. You will paralyze yourself with doubt and fear. For the moment, making no decision will feel safe and comfortable – nothing is farther from the truth. If you religiously execute the Leader AAR on all your big decisions, you will gain experience and instinct. It's important

that you view the failure as a learning event, trust your instincts, and act…quickly.

> *"Courage is going from failure to failure without losing enthusiasm."*
> **Winston Churchill**

3. **Own it** – Assign credit to as many people as you can for your good decisions and take all the blame for your bad ones. If you execute the Leader AAR process honestly, it provides the perfect platform for you to own your failures with your boss, your direct team, and your entire organization. Nothing is more demoralizing and fear inducing in an organization than a leader that deflects accountability, makes excuses, or assigns blame for failures. In the blink of an eye, that fear will turn to mistrust, and if you need a reminder on what mistrust does to leadership – reread Parker Principle #2. On the flip side, nothing builds trust and credibility faster than a leader standing up and holding themselves accountable for failures.

> *"You build on failure. You use it as a stepping stone. Close the door on the past. You don't try to forget the mistakes, but you don't dwell on it. You don't let it have any of your energy, or any of your time, or any of your space."*
> **Johnny Cash**

4. **Sponsor a Culture of Failure** – Okay, I know that sounds bad, but if an organization does not fear failure, then they will risk more, they will fail less, and the organization will deliver better results. Lead with a "Everybody gets a second chance" (except for integrity and ethical issues) mentality. It will not only help you build a results-driven culture powered by innovation and intelligent risk taking, but it will also establish an environment where your people will give you a second chance. I am not suggesting you ignore any bad decisions, mistakes, or failures, but I am suggesting you put it through the failure learning process… then move on.

My last point on the Culture of Failure is don't forget this in how you hire and retain talent. If you witness junior leaders conducting themselves in ways that are detrimental to the culture, give them their "second chance" coaching session, and if the behavior continues – exit them from the organization. No matter how hard you work to establish a failure positive culture – a junior leader can reverse everything by behaving in a manner that causes anger, fear, or resentment, resulting in diminished trust.

On the hiring front, ensure you have two or three questions that probe a candidate's 'failure profile" and keep it simple:

- What have been your three greatest failures?
- What was the actual outcome vs. the expected outcome?
- What did you do or what did you learn?

If the candidate cannot easily name three failures, your warning lights should be activated.

I put this candidate in one of three categories:

1) They do not have enough leadership experience to have experienced failures or they lack courage and are risk averse.
2) They are not self-aware enough to acknowledge their failures – which means they did not learn anything from the failure.
3) They are not being honest with you.

In all cases, your gut should be telling you to walk away from this candidate and don't look back.

"No human ever became interesting by not failing. The more you fail and recover and improve, the better you are as a person. Ever meet someone who's always had everything work out for them with zero struggle? They usually have the depth of a puddle. Or they don't exist."
Chris Hardwick

Courage, Dreams, and Failure, when engaged properly, make a powerful combination that will help a good leader become a great leader. I will leave you with these parting thoughts. Never under estimate the impact that courage has on your ability to lead. Look for opportunities to face fears and build courage. Without courage, you will be severely challenged to make a dream into a reality and any failure into a positive learning opportunity. Use the Big Dream Cycle – Impossible, Improbable then Inevitable. Never fear failure; it is inevitable. Learn from it, grow, tap into your instinct, and move forward.

"Courage doesn't always roar. Sometimes courage is the quiet voice at the end of the day saying, "I will try again tomorrow."
Mary Anne Radmacher

Rangers Lead the Way!

Courageous Leadership
Chapter Recap

- Courage is the Quality that guarantees all others.
- Courage defeats Fear of failure and Fear of leadership inadequacy.
- Face your Fears by taking action.
- Identify and name your most debilitating business fears.
- Understand the source of your fears and engage them.
- Talk about your fears and keep a journal of triggers.
- "The future belongs to those who believe in the beauty of their dreams." – Eleanor Roosevelt
- Unleash the power of your dreams.
- Don't allow doubt in yourself or from others inhibit going after your dreams.
- Failure is the greatest mechanism for learning ever developed in the history of the world.
- Trust your instincts, make a decision, act and fail quickly.
- Sponsor a culture of failure and unlock organizational innovation.

Parker Principle #4

Leadership is Relationships

*"The most important single ingredient in the formula of success is
knowing how to get along with people."*
Theodore Roosevelt

There are several dictionary.com definitions of Leadership, but I want
to focus on two:

1) the position or function of leader, a person who guides or directs a
group.

2) the act or instance of leading, guiding, or directing.

Sounds straightforward and simple, right? Not even close. There are
dozens of variations on the "definition of leadership. If you google
"definition of leadership", you get 124,000 results in .51 seconds. With
the magnitude of these results, we have to accept there is no way we
can read, digest, or apply 124,000 views on what makes an effective
leader. Therefore, for the purposes of our discussion, we will leverage
some commonalities in these definitions.

1) To be a leader, you must have followers.

2) A leader is usually trying to get their followers to do something.

3) These followers are people.

Regardless of what definition you use – people are at the center of all
leadership. A leader must have a relationship with their people to
compel them to accept their guidance, direction, and accomplish any
objective. Leadership is simply the output of the working relationship

between leader and follower. Great leaders understand the requirement for them to build relationships to create high performing teams. Relationships build trust. Think about the closest relationships in your life. If you look deep enough, you will find that the stronger the relationship, the stronger the trust. The same is true with leaders and followers. Connecting with your people is one of the most effective ways for a leader to lead.

Great leaders are always looking for ways to strengthen and maintain relationships with their people. When the leader/follower relationship is founded in trust and confidence, you can unlock the performance potential of an individual or team. The reality is the more senior the leader, the less critical that leader's technical skills become. The senior leader's success becomes more tied to their ability to connect and build relationships. A senior leader's level of success will be determined by what they can get done through others. I am not suggesting a leader does not have to be technically competent, but I am saying technical competence alone will not provide a leader the results they are tasked to deliver. The most powerful quality to building these critical relationships is effective communication.

Communication is:

1) an act or instance of transmitting.
2) a process by which information is exchanged between individuals through a common system of symbols, signs, or behaviors.

Effective communication combines conveyance and reception skills. While it's important for a leader to **convey** their mission, vision, and intention, it's just as important for that leader to **receive** input through actively listening. This is how relationships are built.

"In real life the most practical advice for leaders is to not treat pawns like pawns, nor princes like princes, but all persons like persons."

James MacGregor Burns

Treat people as people, not as jobs, tasks, or outputs. Doing so requires you to take an interest in them, ask questions, and listen attentively. It's all about relationships. A relationship-driven leader empowers others and considers empathy essential to creating a high-performance team. This type of leader also views decision-making through a relationship-focused lens vs. a position or title based power.

Once again, relationship building is a skill that can be learned. While a leader may not change their authentic personality, they can manage and change their behaviors.

Here are some proven best practices that a leader can use to lead through relationships:

- Focus on team member development as much as team member performance.

- Encourage the team to speak openly and honestly. Reward transparency and straight talk. Don't mistake silence or a lack of questions as acceptance or agreement. Dive deep, peel the onion, and engage in two-way communication.

- Ask for opinions and collaborate on issues and important decisions.

- Balance empathy and strong decision making.

- Open yourself up to differing points of view.
- Focus on your Emotional IQ (EQ)– self-awareness, self-regulation, empathy, and social skills.

- Be transparent, direct, and honest, but don't be an A@@!
- Focus on responding to a situation vs reacting.

- Be decisive by building consensus not by directive.

"The best way to lead people into the future is to connect with them deeply in the present."
James Kouzes and Barry Posner

Leadership Connection:

"Building relationships is one of the strongest skills sets related to leadership effectiveness," says Jean Leslie, a researcher at the Center for Creative Leadership(CCL). "Managers with experience building relationships are seen as more effective." That statement emerges from a comprehensive research study undertaken by CCL involving more than 438,000 respondents. Two thirds of respondents said, "building and maintaining relationships is a critical competency."

On an intellectual level, we easily accept the criticality of the relationship competency, but how this manifests as a priority in our everyday behavior as leaders is much more challenging to think about. There is a consistent belief among the talent community that today's leaders, especially senior leaders, are not as adept as they must be at relationship building. According to the CCL – relationship building ranked tenth out of sixteen leadership competencies.

This is a disappointing situation, considering that, in leadership, the strength of relationship building is directly tied to the strength of a leader's influence. Influence rarely makes the top 20 leadership competencies because of its perception as a 'soft skill.' But I submit to you that one of the primary differences between an ordinary leader and a great, upwardly mobile leader is usually influence. There is no way to be effective without influence. The key to influence is relationships, real quality relationships.

"The most useful person in the world today is the man or woman who knows how to get along with other people. Human relations is the most important science in living."
Stanley Allyn

We should all understand the clear distinction between a relationship and a person in our contact list. As a business leader, nothing is more valuable than the quality of your relationships, not the quality of your contact list. More often than we would care to acknowledge, our success as a leader is enhanced or diminished by our ability to establish key relationships and build influence spheres.

We've observed it throughout our careers; the leaders with the greatest influence always have the strongest relationships, and the leaders with the strongest relationships also have the most organizational influence. So how do we build these strong quality relationships? How do we convert these relationships into productive influence that enables us to be better leaders and help us achieve our goals?

"It occurs to me that our survival may depend upon our talking to one another." "It's the people we hardly know, and not our closest friends, who will improve our lives most dramatically"
Meg Jay

Quality Relationships

Quality relationships are:
- Based on character, investment, and adding value to others.
- About trust, service, humility, empathy and care.
- Focused on the commitment of time and energy.
- Connections across generations, philosophies, race, and gender.
- Are planned, purposeful, and intentional.

Whether you dream of occupying the C-Suite, being a Director of a public company, being a published author, or even becoming a highly sought after public speaker, you will need meaningful Quality Relationships. Quality Relationships generate influence. Before we get into best practices for establishing, nurturing, and sustaining Quality Relationships, I want to talk about networking and making initial contacts.

> *"Networking is not about just connecting people. It's about connecting people with people, people with ideas, and people with opportunities."*
> **Michele Jennae**

Networking

So often throughout my career, I have seen talented people miss tremendous opportunities to develop Quality Relationships. They have the errant belief that relationship building is a functional tool used to help them achieve their personal objectives. They look at this principle as "what's in it for me?" and not "what can I do for someone else?"

At its core, this belief is grounded in a mercenary type selfishness that brings with it a cloud of negativity, suspicion, and cynicism i.e., "If this person can't help me today or tomorrow, I don't want to waste my precious time or resources building the relationship." This self-serving belief is usually an unhealthy extension of a dream.

We are human. We may be lured by the romantic belief that one day we will have that magical introduction to the career changing person who simply by strength of touch will make all our career dreams come true.

I like to call this the *"Midas Touch Delusion."* Unfortunately, this delusion is not a viable strategy for initiating and building Quality Relationships. The delusion can create behaviors that counter career progression or lead to career stagnation. Idling and waiting on Midas to come along and make your dreams come true, rather than working hard to create your own success, is an ineffective strategy, one many people take, and the vast majority have found to fail.

> *"The true value of networking doesn't come from how many people we can meet but rather how many people we can introduce to others."*
> **Simon Sinek**

While these bad behaviors happen every day, they usually manifest themselves in their purest form during networking opportunities, such as dinners, charity events, conferences etc., when people swarm around those who they feel can give their career a leg up.

We've all seen or experienced these bad behaviors. I have seen them so often over my career that I have given names to the most common ones. I think you will also recognize each behavior from your life experiences.

See if any of these individuals look familiar:

The Floater

A.K.A Transactional Terry: The mathematician that sincerely believes connections are a simple numbers game. The more connections, the better. They are on a single-minded mission to meet as many people as possible at a networking event, and during that time, they are completely in transactional mode.

They spend the minimum time with each transaction, just long enough to not be rude but not long enough to make any real connection. How can you spot them? They are talking to you with their mouths, while glancing over your shoulder to identify their next target. What's frightening is that I've actually seen this technique recommended as a best practice for networking:

"Although you want to build strong relationships with your networking contacts, the goal is to meet as many people as possible when you're at networking events," says an article on *MasterMind Connections* – a site led by business coach, Chad Coe.

"Ask questions and, presuming you see a fit, politely ask for their card and ask for permission to stay in touch," states Coe. *"Remember, this is not the time to make a sales presentation or to tell your life story. It is the time to spend a few minutes of quality time with someone new and then move on to meet a new prospect."*

Inside Secret: Here's a tip from an old pro…We always know when we are being transacted. I don't feel warm and fuzzy about a person that views me as a prospect or transaction. Here are my poker tells – Poker Tell#1 "Oh no! I have just run out of business cards. I'm so sorry. But feel free to give me yours." If you hear me saying this to someone, guess what is NOT going to happen? Yeah, I won't be reaching out any time soon…or ever!

Don't be Transactional Terry

The Business Card Ninja

AKA Nina/Nino Ninja: They are actually worse than the floaters because they won't even take the time to pretend they are trying to make a connection. Their mission is to exchange or collect as many business cards as possible during the event. They lead with their business card, thrusting it at you with the blinding speed of a Ninja's knife.

If you are lucky enough to avoid the paper cut, then you get the cold expectant stare, demanding you to reciprocate. My response is typically a rinse and repeat from above – "Sorry, ……" Don't call me, I'll call you!

Poker Tell #2: Where I store your business card will indicate whether you have made a successful connection. If you go in my right jacket pocket, then you made no genuine impression on me and your card is likely headed for the shredder. If you make the left jacket pocket, the heart is on the left side, then you have made the initial cut, and now it is up to you to stoke the relationship fire.

Every once in a while, you have an interaction with a person where you feel the protocols and chemistry are all aligned. You actually feel like you want to help them. In those rare cases, I take things a step further and put their card in my wallet. When this happens, it means I hope we can connect again and help if I can. Like I said, this is very rare – maybe 2 or 3 times in a year.

To recap:
- Right Jacket Pocket = Shredder
- Left Jacket Pocket = Neutral but open. Waiting for your next step
- Wallet = You made an impression and I want to help.

Now let's meet a few more "right pocket" people:

The Interrogator:
- Zero preparation and knows nothing about you. This is the person who asks you question after question like you are in an interrogation room. You leave the conversation exhausted.

The Intimidator:
- They physically barge into a conversation and, either through body positioning or by monopolizing the conversation, bully everybody else away.

The Salesman:

- You get the canned elevator speech right before they try to close. Nothing is more irritating than someone you just met trying to close you. Right pocket all the way.

The Liar:

- "Pete gave me your name and told me to reach out to you at this event." Sooner or later, I will talk to Pete. If you lied, you will now have burned two bridges forever – both me and Pete.

And last but not least!

The Taker

- "Excuse me, Sir, can you spare some change?" Before they have added a single ounce of value to the relationship, they are asking for a favor. Why should I do something for you before I even know your name? Right pocket.

All these "right pocket" behaviors create a very transactional environment that inhibits your ability to make a quality connection that could have transformed into a Quality Relationship.

> *"A really important part of networking is actually about what you bring – not just what you want to get out of it. Contribution is a big part of networking success."*
> **Gina Romero**

I try to focus on some simple fundamental tenets to help me avoid being lured into the transactional trap. I believe they offer you the best chance of transitioning a simple networking connection into a lasting Quality Relationship.

- **Focus on Quality Not Quantity**: Making two real connections at an event is better than collecting two dozen business cards through transient connection.

- **Ditch the Sales Pitch**: Never try to "close" someone right after you meet them. Don't ask for anything other than the opportunity to connect again.

- **Who Cares?**: Don't assume others should care about your problems or needs. No one cares, and no one should care until you show them you genuinely care about them or their needs.

- **Avoid the Me, Me, Me and Me**: The foundation of a Quality Relationship is the ability for each person to add value to the other person's life. If all you talk about is YOU during your connection, then it is highly unlikely you are trying to figure out how to add value to another person's world.

- **Be Realistic:** While the old Air Force slogan "Aim High" has a certain romantic draw, when networking, it should be Aim Real.

- **Don't Aim Too High**: Remember, Quality Relationships are mutually beneficial. While we all would love to connect with Bill Gates, Mark Zuckerberg or Michael Dell, you must be clear on what value you bring to the relationship and how you can help the other person in the relationship meet their needs.

"What makes networking work is that it sets up win-win situations in which all parties involved get to take something home. Networking is a sharing process. Until you understand that, you won't have much of a network."
Earl G. Graves, Sr.

The Work

You are now connection savvy, and over time, you have worked hard and made some left pocket and maybe even wallet connections. What do you do now? How do you turn a genuine connection into a Quality Relationship? How do you turn Quality Relationships into influence? You start by insuring you are in a "give, give, give" mentality.

Your sole focus must be:

- What can I give this person?
- How can I help them?
- How can I add value to their lives?

That's it - **no exceptions**. Plan to invest time, energy, and maybe even money to figure out how to help this person.

Frankly, this is where most people check out and fail. Quality Relationships require a great amount of effort and commitment. It's not easy, but nothing worthwhile ever is. Quality Relationships take years of investment to build and nurture; they are powerful and can sometimes mean the difference between being asked to lead an organizational restructure or being asked to leave through an organizational restructure.

Therefore, the question becomes, how do you transform genuine connections into a powerful sphere of Quality Relationships? The answer is in preparation. I firmly believe we either plan to succeed or plan to fail. Taking time on the front end to ensure you are moving forward effectively will help strongly increase your chances of success on the back end. To that goal, let's take a moment to dig into some of the more effective preparation strategies I have implemented over the years.

Preparation Best Practices Include:

1) **Prepare a Strategy:** Quality Relationships are purposeful, planned, and intentional. Take the time to assess your entire situation.

Where are you in your career today?
What are your endpoint objectives?

Identify and make a list of the people in the universe that are not current relationships, who could help you achieve your objectives. Objectively review that list and divide it into two distinct groups.

Priority 1 – the people on the list you could assist or provide value to their careers or lives.
Priority 2 – all remaining.

The Priority 1 list will be your focus for establishing Quality Relationships. However, this does not mean you should forget about the individuals on your Priority 2 list. Make sure you review the Priority 2 list periodically to assess whether there is a name that could now be moved to Priority 1.

The Universe of People

Priority – 1U   Priority – 2U

Priority-1U: All the people in the universe that can help you achieve your goals and you CAN reciprocate.

Priority-2U: All the people in the universe that can help you reach your goals and you can NOT reciprocate at this time.

2) **Assess Current Relationships** – Carefully review each relationship and confirm whether they qualify for Priority 1 or 2. Now review your relationships and identify the people that may have one or two degrees of separation from a person in your Priority 1 group. People that can make a key introduction.

These people will now become your Priority 3 group.

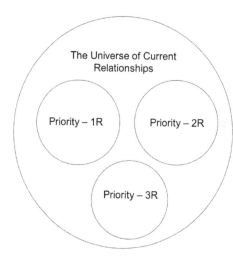

Priority-1R: All current relationships that can help you achieve your goals and you CAN reciprocate.

Priority-2R: All current relationships that can help you reach your goals and you can NOT reciprocate at this time.

Priority-3R: All current relationships that have one or two degrees of separation from a member in your Priority-1 group.

"Networking is simply the cultivating of mutually beneficial, give and take, win-win relationships. It works best, however, when emphasizing the "give" part."
Bob Burg

Engagement Best Practices:

You can now create the target list to execute engagement best practices.

Priority(1U) + Priority(1R) + Priority(3R) = Total Priority 1 List

Leverage the following engagement best practices with the individuals in Total Priority 1 list, with the simple objective of establishing Quality Relationships.

1) Approach the relationship solely to add value to the other person's life. Reject the "what's in it for me?' attitude as you purposely focus on the other party. What can you do or give to assist their career or dreams?

2) Be prepared to invest the time and effort. Give freely and be accessible.

3) Be transparent and authentic. No name dropping, exaggeration, or lying.

4) Make a case for building a relationship by identifying shared values and goals, then work on consistency to develop mutual respect.

5) Be Likable. Smile, sincerely listen, and exchange personal stories. Doing so will help you ask great questions and internalize unique pieces of information.

6) Share Vulnerability. This establishes our authentic self and helps to build trust. This is best shared with a select few, and I encourage you to keep this circle small. Shared vulnerability connects right into loyalty and conveys the clear message of "I trust you and always got your back."

7) Use technology to combat the chaos of life. Execute a disciplined "stay connected" strategy. Leverage note taking and contact relationship management software to help you stay organized. The point is, do whatever it takes to stay focused and stay on top of these new relationships.

"All the time and effort put into networking can be all for naught if there is no follow-through. The same goes for sales. And leadership, And well, everything."
Beth Ramsay

Here is what I want you to remember. No one advances, wins, or gets promoted on their own. It happens through developing Quality Relationships. I have seen and experienced this phenomenon time and time again throughout my career, both positive and negative. I have lost a promotion to a peer, when on paper, I had more experience, ran a larger business, delivered better results, and had a skill set that was a better fit for the role. After I lost the role, I went to the hiring executive to do my personal AAR. The conversation went something like this:

"Bill, the interviews went so well, we had great chemistry, you liked my experience, past performance and results. It would help my professional development if I understood why I was not your guy. I have tough skin, so I really want the cold hard truth."

His answer was sobering. His summarized response was: "This is a critical role. The person in the role can make or break my career. On paper and even with your references, you are by far the optimal person for the role. However, I know "Jack." I trust Jack and he won't let me down"

Wow! Sometimes, the truth hurts, but the truth is the truth. This was transformational for me. Until that point in my career, I always believed that, if I outworked and outperformed my peers in every aspect, that would be enough. I recognized that I had never seen relationship building as critical or even important. This is business. We have stakeholders and shareholders. It's all about delivering revenue and profits, being ethical, taking care of your people and your customers. Where does building relationships fit into that paradigm? I learned the hard way the flaw in this mindset. It was a powerful lesson.

Trust is a powerful influencer and trust is one output of a Quality Relationship.

Lesson learned, **relationships matter.**

Finally, to be fair, "Jack" delivered well for "Bill". He stepped up and did not let him down. To Bill, this proved he made the right choice and was right to trust his experience and relationship with the Jack.

> *"To be successful, you have to be able to relate to people; they have to be satisfied with your personality to be able to do business with you and to build a relationship with mutual trust."*
> **George Ross**

The hard truth, especially for senior leaders, is there are a lot of talented leaders who consistently deliver superior performances. Usually, the final candidates for a senior role are all great leaders with great resumes. When the competition is that intense, Quality Relationships can be the key differentiator. My story about Bill and Jack is an example of how a direct Quality Relationship can "win the day." But there is also power in what I call "special" Quality Relationships – Coaches, Mentors, Advocates, and Champions.

Coaches, Mentors, Advocates and Champions

These are special types of Quality Relationships that each have a unique role and responsibility within your influence sphere.

Coaches – This is the baseline, or foundational, Quality Relationship. A coach is willing to dedicate the time, effort, and energy to helping you become a better leader. This person might be part of your organization, but their goal is to assist you as you develop and grow. They are focused on maximizing your performance. A coach is both a confidant and advisor. This relationship is based on trust and a maximum level of transparency. You should be able to bring all your performance challenges to your coach and openly receive feedback. A coach may be able to teach you new hard or soft skills. While maintaining this Quality Relationship is important, they are most powerful when you need a new skill, entering a new function or department.

Mentors – Mentors act as sounding boards, offering advice as needed and guidance as requested. They offer a more holistic type of support than a coach and expect little in return. This person should be inside your organization and not in your direct chain of command. A mentor will help you understand and navigate your organization. While the relationship with a mentor is usually not as deep as what you will experience with a Coach, it is still based on trust and mutual respect. A mentor will usually connect you with their network and offer their experience and advice to help navigate your career. While sometimes you may outgrow the technical expertise that a Coach provides, you will never outgrow the Mentor relationship. It's indefinite.

Advocate – Sometimes called a Sponsor, there are prerequisites for someone to be an Advocate.

They are:

- Within your company
- A level or two above you
- Have title, stature, and influence
- They have something to gain by sponsoring your success

Just to be clear, being a top performer is mandatory to have a chance of finding an Advocate. Advocates view you as a protégé and have a vested interest in your success. They will offer guidance and critical feedback because they believe in you. This person will openly advocate for you. They will readily talk about your strengths and rarely talk about your weaknesses. There are two kinds of advocates, active and passive. Both are critical to success but for two different reasons. We will talk about them in more detail later.

Champion – This person is basically an Advocate that **IS NOT** in your organization. The same rules as Advocate apply. They should be 1 to 2 levels above you, have current or past title, stature, and influence. A Champion always has your back for advice, connections, guidance, or even a reference. A Champion is a person that, if they get a reference call on you out of the blue with no notification or preparation, you don't worry about what they will say... because they always have your back. While this is probably the least intimate of the four special Quality Relationships, it is powerful, and you never know when you need a Champion for an outside role or board seat.

Important Note!

Remember the Priority Groups we discussed earlier? Every person that is in one of these four special Quality Relationships should be a part of your Total Priority 1 group. This will allow you to figure out how to engage them and nurture the relationship. You must put in the work. You should have 1 or 2 Mentors and as many Advocates as you can win. When the rubber meets the road, the Advocates decide your fate and your future

"Networking with integrity creates a greater willingness of all parties to be part of a human conduit to serve as energy and resource to one another. Sometimes you will give more than you receive and sometimes you will get back more than you give. It's not about keeping score."
Chris London

Mentors and Advocates (Active and Passive) Business Reviews

I want to dive a little deeper around these three critical relationships and how they can make or break your career. As a senior leader, I have always committed to a Quarterly Business Review(QBR) with my boss. Depending on the size of the business I ran, the review could be 1 hour to 4 hours. After the review, I would use the next 90 days to "go on tour."

First, I would set up an hour with my mentors (usually only 1 or 2). This meant reducing a 3 hour QBR deck to a 40-minute Mini QBR deck. Remember, the Mentor relationship is based on trust and vulnerability, so I would take off all my armor and take them through my mini QBR, both the good and the bad. I would get their insights and advice on what was working great and what could I do to improve. I would then share with my Mentor the remaining targets of my tour(Advocates) and a version of the mini QBR I prepared for them. Finally, I would then incorporate their insights and advice into the rest of my tour.

Be advised, getting Advocates on the tour for the first time is a long, tough, and risky process. By design, you are targeting 1 to 2 levels above you, and that can be dicey if you don't have a supportive boss. Often, you don't know who your Advocates are, so you must make an educated guess and ask for the meeting.

Early on, I tried to be strategic and target only 1 or 2 potential Advocates. I quickly learned how important it was to expand my Advocate list to 5 or 10. If an executive 2 levels above me was willing to give me time on their calendar to review my business, I took it. Not just my line leaders but also the senior functional leaders. For example, in one role, every quarter, I took the General Counsel through my mini QBR. You will be surprised by the number of senior executives that will give you 30 minutes on their calendar if you just ask.

102

After getting insight and advice from my Mentor, I went on my Advocate tour. This is a 30-minute meeting, with a 15-minute Mini QBR, and full armor on. An advocate wants to know they are putting their name on a top performer and rising star, so your results on the business review must be stellar. To achieve this, I focused on presenting a 15-minute rock star business review, then spent the next 15 minutes trying to engage on a more personal level- family, hobbies, sports whatever. If they don't kick you out right after the business review, Success! If you can get buy in to get on their calendar for next quarter – Double Success! The idea is to make this a Quality Relationship that can help you grow and develop your own leadership skill set.

Now you have a rhythm. One time, I was coming out of a Senior Executive office after a review when I ran into one of that executive's peers. The executive told him about our quarterly review and how it gave him insights and perspective at the operational level. And just like that, the peer said it sounded like a good idea; why don't I schedule time on his calendar to do a mini QBR. BAM! My purposeful action on the front end paid off in an impactful way that I didn't see coming.

Active Advocates vs Passive Advocates

Mel, you still have not talked about how you differentiate between active and passive Advocates. Honestly, for the "Mel Tour," I don't differentiate. Instead, I give all potential Advocates the same Mel mini QBR. All Advocates are awesome, but not all are created equal.

Let me share this real world example I experienced personally.

Picture a Board Room, with a huge rectangular table seating 15 or so senior executives. It's a strategy meeting where the business needs a restructure. At this time, the decision has been made to reduce three separate business units down to one. These 3 Business units are being led by 3 General Managers (Mike, Ike, and Bill) and their staff will now become 1 much larger business unit with only one GM. The conversation comes down to which GM will lead the new consolidated business unit and what two GM's would go home.

The executives review each GM's numbers and their Talent development profiles. Then the floor is opened for discussion. One executive points out that Mike seems to be the most qualified, his numbers are excellent, he is well-respected and a great leader (Advocate). Then another voice at the table claims Ike also has great numbers, has been at the company longer, and successfully led us through the last acquisition (Advocate).

Two Active Advocates at work for their protégés. And each makes a strong point. Then the question, does anyone else at the table have an opinion about Mike or Ike? A third executive now weighs in: "Yeah, I sit down with Ike about once a quarter to review his business. He seems really buttoned up and you can't argue with his performance. I like him." (Passive Advocate)

I am not certain about the deciding factor, but Ike got the job and Mike and Bill were removed in the restructure. Clearly, Bill never had a chance as he had no Advocates in the room. While Mike had an active advocate, which is awesome, it still is trumped by the combination of active and passive advocates.

- Active Advocates will openly and without prompting support you.
- Passive Advocates have a good opinion of you if someone asks for that opinion.

"Don't wait until you desperately need a social network to begin developing one."
Frank Sonnenberg

Postscript: As I stated, Ike got the job, but Mike did not go home. Mike's Advocate found him a position on his team. The role was probably not as prestigious as Ike's, but it was a damn good role. Bill started to scramble and reach out to many people for help, but it was too late. You would be shocked at the number of people that get on my calendar for the first time, and the purpose of the meeting is to ask for help. Unfortunately, it is always too late once the decision has been made.

Two lessons: 1) You can never have enough Advocates, and 2) Don't be Bill.

> *"Networking is an enrichment program, not an entitlement program."*
> **Susan RoAne**

The importance of Quality Relationships and relationship building skills should never be underestimated. You must make the time as a Leader to develop relationships with your people. It is just as important that you make the time to increase your sphere of influence with Quality Relationships. Be targeted as you work to create as much Advocacy as you can, especially 2 levels or above.

Leadership is Relationships
Chapter Recap

- Effective communication is critical to establish and maintain healthy relationships.
- Relationship building is a skill that can be learned.
- Leadership effectiveness is directly related to your effectiveness in building relationships.
- Focus on building Quality Relationships.
- Networking savvy is the single best platform to initiate new relationships.
- Networking Best Practices
    o Focus on quality not quantity.
    o Avoid me, me, me.
    o Ditch the sales pitch.
- Quality Relationship require work – prepare a strategy.
- Assess current relationships.
- Leverage relationship engagement best practices.
- Understand and leverage special Quality Relationships.
    o Coach
    o Mentor
    o Advocates
    o Champions

Parker Principle #5:

Be a Great Listener

"I only wish I could find an institute that teaches people how to listen. Business people need to listen at least as much as they need to talk. Too many people fail to realize that real communication goes in both directions."
Lee Iacocca

Being a great listener is probably one of the most underrated and under developed fundamentals of Take The Limits Off Leadership. It is the most powerful skill for connecting with people, customers, peers, family, and friends. It's been my experience that great leadership is established by the ability to connect with the people you lead, and it is virtually impossible to connect with the people you lead without listening to them.

Just because a person is an eloquent speaker or an effective presenter doesn't mean they will be great leaders.

Great Leaders are also Great Listeners!

"Of all the skills of leadership, listening is the most valuable—and one of the least understood. Most captains of industry listen only sometimes, and they remain ordinary leaders. But a few, the great ones, never stop listening. That's how they get word before anyone else of unseen problems and opportunities."
Peter Nulty

Great Leaders have a deeper level of understanding of the lives and situations affecting the people they lead. This level of understanding only comes from listening to people. It can't be gained from an individual perspective.

In today's ultra-connected world, you must be able to leverage every format and medium of communication as an opportunity to listen. I know that sounds incongruent with a reality where we can become engrossed in our texts, tweets, and chats, a reality where we often fail to connect and communicate with people that are in the same room. But connecting is essential to great leadership.

Previously, we talked about great leaders having a unique mosaic of both innate and learned skills. For most of us, being a good listener isn't one of the innate skills; it just doesn't come naturally. Great listeners usually have a wide range of learned skills and best practices they employ naturally and instinctively. These skills can be practiced, refined, and strengthened over time, but they are skills nonetheless. I don't dare consider myself a "great listener" but I commit to working my butt off every day to develop and hone my listening skills.

And, while I may never reach the designation of Master Listener, I do believe I'm a better leader because I put in the work every day to become a better listener. I would like to share what I've learned on my journey (both successes and failures), and in the process, provide you with some insights, tools and best practices, so we can all strive to become "Masters of Listening."

"To learn through listening, practice it naively and actively. Naively means that you listen openly, ready to learn something, as opposed to listening defensively, ready to rebut. Listening actively means you acknowledge what you heard and act accordingly."
Betsy Sanders

Below, you will find a short list of fundamentals that have proven critical during my journey. In my experience, a good listening skill set requires knowledge, techniques, and practice.

Here are some places I suggest we start to build a great listening skill set:

- **Be Attentive**: Focus on the words coming out of the other person's mouth. Then process those words, think about what they mean and how they apply to your world. If you are in your own head, anxiously waiting for a chance to make a brilliant point or counterpoint, then it is highly unlikely you are listening to the other person.

"Most people do not listen with the intent to understand; they listen with the intent to reply."
Stephen R. Covey

- **Body Language (Physicality) Counts**: Relax, make good eye contact, lean forward, and open your body. This means no crossed arms or legs. You should also be purposeful about removing any physical obstacles between you and the speaker i.e., computer screens, desks, tables, backpacks, or plants.

  Come from behind the desk or the table. Pull up a chair directly across from the speaker. In the military, we would call this getting "knee to knee." The physical environment and body language are critical considerations that are "easy" best practices to improve listening.

- **Be Courteous**: Put down whatever you are doing and give the other person your full attention. You should make a point to never:
  - Interrupt or Yawn
  - Look at your watch or check your phone
  - Look over the other person's shoulder for either someone more interesting to talk to or for help to save you from your current conversation
  - Show shock or dismay at what is being said
  - Rush the person by asking closed end questions

"You cannot truly listen to anyone and do anything else at the same time."
M. Scott Peck

- **Silence or Mute the ME-ME:** A conversation between two people is not just a single conversation. There are actually three conversations occurring simultaneously. The conversation between You and Me, the internal conversation happening in your mind (You-You), and the internal conversation happening in my mind (Me-Me).

  Me-Me conversations include: Man, traffic was bad today. My wife's birthday is coming up. I have three more conference calls today. My feet hurt. I'm hungry. I wonder if my boss will yell at me today? Is a meteor headed toward earth? Why am I here...

  Wait! What did YOU just say?

  At any given moment, our random and raging thoughts can interfere with our ability to listen. While I haven't reached the Zen mastery of silencing the Me-Me, with practice, I've gotten good at reducing the volume. I focus on understanding each word and sentence and then analyzing them for emotional content and meaning. The more I focus, the lower the Me-Me volume.

- **Show you Care:** Show interest and empathy. Ask clarifying questions, repeat interesting points, be sincere and authentic. Provide thoughtful feedback.

  But, there is a catch!

110

To do this, you must care about what the other person is saying. If you don't care...it shows! And in a big way!

If you can't give the person your full attention, then it is far better to disengage in a polite manner. Something like: "Excuse me for a moment. I think I see my future spouse over there", is a far better option than rudely faking your way through the interaction and wasting everyone's time and good will.

As you listen, try to empathize with their position, but do not patronize. People can tell when you are talking down to them, and if you don't want to know the answer to a question, don't ask! Nothing is more demoralizing than for someone to ask about your daughter's soccer skills or your son's saxophone lessons then watch them disengage halfway through your answer. It damages respect and trust, sometimes irreversibly.

"One of the most sincere forms of respect is actually listening to what another has to say."
Bryant H. McGill

- **Check your Attitude:** Don't approach a conversation with prejudgment or a pre-formed opinion of what you believe the other person will say. This approach could cause you to not hear the actual words being said, or to misinterpret the words being said based on a preformed bias. Keep an open mind and don't be defensive. Instead, be comfortable with being uncomfortable. All subject matter of a conversation may not be interesting or align with your world view, but you can't allow it to prevent you from being a great listener.

- **Confidentiality**: As my grandmother always said, "No one likes a gossip!" The easiest way to destroy the connection built by being a great listener is to not be mature enough to respect the confidentiality of shared information. I won't even mention the bad Karma in store for the intrepid and untrustworthy soul that uses shared confidential information for anything other than good. Betrayal has an expensive price tag.

- **Leverage Technology (Remember the Alamo):** There is no better way to be a great listener than to remember the details of a conversation and share them back when relevant. This can mean during the same interaction or later. Now, I realize this is easier said than done. Personally, while I clearly understand the importance of remembering, if it is not a number, fact, or figure my memory is just shy of horrible. So, I am predisposed to fail as a great listener.

Well, now what? Do I just give up listening as a lost cause? Never!

Instead, I break Rule#1 with an apology and pull out my iPhone. I tell the individual I am speaking with that my memory is horrible but what they are saying is so important I want to remember everything. Is it okay if I capture a few quick notes?

I've learned that an apology and asking permission to take a few notes can be a little uncomfortable in that moment. But when I remember their spouses name, anniversary date, the fact that Sarah plays soccer, Ron plays the saxophone or that they grew up in Canada, it pays dividends. People have a certain look that comes over their face when they recognize they were important and respected enough for me to listen and remember the details about their lives. That look that makes a little initial discomfort and awkwardness a small price to pay.

"Listening is a magnetic and strange thing, a creative force. The friends who listen to us are the ones we move toward. When we are listened to, it creates us, makes us unfold and expand."
Karl A. Menniger

When making notes on a specific conversation, I use the Notes App on my phone. It doesn't need to be anything fancy. Instead, I usually step over beside them as I am typing, so they see my notes, and I involve them in my note taking process. Did I spell your spouse's name right? Is that anniversary date correct? Sarah is 5, right?

I believe sharing the process with them will grab their attention and show them that, while I am breaking rule#1, it is all about them. I am still engaged, and they have my full focus.

Once a week, I take these notes and input them into a great contact management software. I use Contacts CRM (Apple App Store). I set key dates, birthdays, and anniversaries to pop up as reminders. I then try to send a quick note on that day and include any other information I captured. Happy Anniversary to you and Jane. How are the kids? Sarah still in love with soccer?

Every time, no exceptions, I get a kind response, and often times, I get a new piece of information to add to the contact. Jane just started a new job; Sarah is now into basketball. It takes a lot of work but the connection, positive energy, and good karma you put into the world is worth every minute. Try it. I guarantee results. If not, cup of coffee on me.

- **I REALLY have something to say syndrome:** It is challenging, if not impossible, to be listening to the person speaking when interrupting or talking over them. Normally, that means you have transitioned from listening mode to formulation mode.

In formulation mode, you have an overwhelming desire to say something, and you are busy in your own head with a Me-Me conversation. Your focus has changed to making a brilliant point or a counterpoint, asking an insightful question, or telling a phenomenally funny or interesting story. In these moments, many individuals feel like they physiologically need to say what is racing through their mind.

There is a natural human need to be heard, but giving in to this need means you can't possibly be listening. Think about it. When someone is speaking and they are interrupted, you think, "Well that's just rude!" And you are right; it is rude. But that moment was likely caused by someone not listening to what was going on around them. They are so locked in the Me-Me conversation they are having in their head that they do not realize what they have done until it's too late.

"The best time to hold your tongue is the time you feel you must say something or bust."
Josh Billings

We all must guard against the volume of the Me-Me conversation. You ever notice in a meeting, town hall, or conference Q&A that people ask questions that have just been asked and answered? This is because they were lost in the Me-Me while waiting their turn. They were so focused on preparing what they needed to ask that they never even realized their mistake until people turn and give them the, "Dang, are you stupid or something" look. We have all been on the receiving end of that look. Be aware and be on guard.

"This is the problem with dealing with someone who is actually a good listener. They don't jump in on your sentences, saving you from actually finishing them, or talk over you, allowing what you do manage to get out to be lost or altered in transit. Instead, they wait, so you have to keep going."
Sarah Dessen

Guard Against Poor Listening Skills

Poor listening skills are stealthy and sneaky. They are difficult to recognize and they tend to creep up when you least expect it. In my journey, I have put these poor listening skills in three distinct buckets: **Superficial Listening, Corporate Listening, and Husband Listening**

- **Superficial Listening** is simply listening at the periphery of comprehension while still giving many of the physical signs of active listening, like eye contact, nodding in affirmation, and the insidious "right." But literally, this type of listening should probably be called the great fake out listening.

  The body seems to listen, but the mind is gone elsewhere (Me-Me). Instead of focusing on the conversation, you are mentally processing through tasks left to do that day, family vacation, friends, sports, weather.... Whatever can scroll through your brain, rather than the conversation at hand.

  In these situations, the mind is processing internal information in lieu of external input.

  When you get totally lost in the volume of Me-Me, you unconsciously stop exhibiting the fake out physical ques.

Suddenly, the person speaking notices and stops talking, clearly expecting some type of response. Then, after a few moments of silence, your mind finally realizes the external input has stopped and you snap back into the present.

The bad part? The person you are supposed to be listening to is now staring at you expectantly, while you scramble to offer a valid response to a question or comment you didn't actually hear. So now you panic. You either take a leap of desperation and attempt to use the fragmented clues you can piece together for an acceptable response, or you realize there is no way out and you capitulate, "Uh, I missed that; can you repeat it please?"

This type of listening is deadly to building any type of relationship. You may be perceived as rude, arrogant, or even lacking simple courtesy and professionalism, all of which are detrimental to trust and can devastate any real connection opportunity.

- **Corporate Listening** is basically a sophisticated type of superficial listening. You are still listening at the periphery of comprehension, but you have developed key trigger points, meaning either words, statements, tone changes or pauses by the speaker that trigger you to move from superficial listening mode into active listening mode.

You have trained your mind to listen for triggers and warnings that snap your attention back to focus in on what is being said.

We do this in lectures, meetings, conferences, and even one on ones. Depending on how sophisticated your triggers are, along with your ability to re-engage into active listening, you may find some level of success with this approach. However, it's just like driving over the speed limit. You may get away with it a lot, but sooner or later, you get a ticket. Depending on the circumstances of when you get caught, there will be a price to pay. Be on guard.

- Finally, we have a skill set I call **Husband Listening** – which is basically a hybrid of Superficial and Corporate listening, but with its own special twist.

First, I think I should shout out an apology to all the husbands around the world; our secret is out. This listening is the most complicated and sometimes the most embarrassing. As a husband for a quarter of a century, I take great pride in the mastery of my husband listening!

You know the scene. Dee and I are in the bedroom. We will clearly be late for the movie, and Dee is still getting dressed. I am sitting on the bed, trying not to make things worse by updating her on the time every thirty seconds or "standing watch" over her, trying to "will" her to move faster. So, I enhance my waiting Zen by whipping out my iPhone. Dee is talking about her day, what happened at the gym, or the last charity luncheon or whatever. Of course, I am texting, getting updates on sports scores, checking the latest news on my CNN app…in other words, actively engaged in a half dozen mind numbing activities while engaging my husband listening and sending out the occasional and timely, "Wow! Really? Oh no! No way. That's crazy! WHAAAAT!?!?"

Honestly, I have a great compliment of responses I masterfully deploy with great precision. Then…it happens. Somewhere at the edge of my consciousness a warning signal sounds, and I realize she has stopped talking.

Uh Oh. Warning lights flash, and I immediately snap back into the right now. I look up and there she is standing in all her wonderful glory, with her hands on her hips, and "the look" on her face. Then the duel starts, me Luke Skywalker vs. her Darth Vader.

"What were you doing?"

"Nothing!"

"You were doing something!"

"No sweetheart, I was listening to you."

"Really? What was the last thing I said?" There it is ....the test! But, like the skilled husband listener that I am, I access the tape in my head, and without a thought, automatically and accurately replay the last moments of the conversation.

BAAMMM!

I am not sure what I just said, but clearly, it is accurate because the hands come off the hips, and she slowly shakes her head side to side, amazed by my prowess, before turning to head towards the door. With an internal high five and a Hooorah!! shout of victory, I dutifully fall in behind her.

After a few steps, I wonder "what did I just say?" I recounted her words accurately (word for word), but I have no idea what I just said or agreed to.

I was not listening, but I am a Jedi master of husband listening.

Over the decades, there have been a few downsides to husband listening, such as agreeing to a vacation in Costa Rica, to purchasing a new expensive pair of shoes with red bottoms, and even the ultimate insult as an Airborne Ranger – agreeing to buying a miniature pinscher toy dog, named Darwin. Yes, you heard me correctly. So, husbands, sons, and males beware. Husband listening can come back to haunt you, even when you attain master status!

In summary:

- Be diligent about practicing and honing your good listening skills.
- Stop talking, concentrate, and pay attention – Silence the Me-Me.
- Make eye contact, interact while having both patience and empathy.
- Guard against all types of poor listening skills – corporate, superficial, and husband.

It may seem like a lot, but doing these things will increase your ability to connect, engage, and influence. Your success and effectiveness as a leader will improve in direct proportion to your ability to be a Great Listener.

"The most basic of all human needs is the need to understand and be understood. The best way to understand people is to listen to them."
Ralph G. Nichols

Can you hear me?

Be a Great Listener
Chapter Recap

- Listening skills are powerful, underrated, and underdeveloped in most leaders.

- Engage great listening best practices.
    o Be attentive
    o Understand and leverage body language
    o Be Courteous
    o Silence or mute the ME-ME
    o Show that you care
    o Leverage technology

- Guard against poor listening skills.
    o Superficial listening
    o Corporate listening
    o Husband listening

Parker Principle #6

No Excuses - Own Your Power

"You must take personal responsibility. You cannot change the circumstances, the seasons, or the wind, but you can change yourself."
Jim Rohn

Take Responsibility!

From a very young age, one of the most profound lessons my grandmother taught me was to take responsibility for my actions. As a Parker Principle and Leadership Force Multiplier, I have evolved this foundational concept into a simple mobilizing theme: Take responsibility for everything in Your Life, No Excuses, and Own Your Power.

When we make excuses about where we are in our careers or project blame for not achieving our dreams onto an external factor "outside of my control," we surrender our power. We cede our destiny and dreams to uncertainty, chance, and coincidence.

Throughout my career, I have seen the inability of leaders to take responsibility for their actions or situations as a debilitating obstacle to their success.

"Success on any major scale requires you to accept responsibility . . . In the final analysis, the one quality that all successful people have is the ability to take on responsibility."
Michael Korda

I am not here to suggest that taking the road of full responsibility is an easy journey. Living with a No Excuses mentality requires arduous and backbreaking work. Deciding to Own Your Power can be awkward and a little unsettling. A leader has to resist the soothing siren's song of comfort that comes from abdicating their responsibility and power. You must be willing to accept risk and put in the work. It's fortunate for all of us leaders that there are milestones and waypoints along the road of responsibility. These checkpoints validate that we Own our Power and live with a No Excuses mindset.

Acceptance

At some point, there must be acceptance. Specifically, acceptance that everything you are or ever will be is entirely within your control – within your Power. It doesn't matter whether it's your personal or professional life, accept that we all have free will and the ability to make decisions. We must be responsible for everything in our lives, Good, Bad, Success, Failure, Happiness and Sadness. Acceptance means we will never surrender our power to anything or anyone. Acceptance means we will never make excuses or assign blame to anyone else. We Own It!

> *"Eventually we all have to accept full and total responsibility for our actions, everything we have done, and have not done."*
> Hubert Selby Jr.

Courage and Fearlessness

You can never really Own Your Power if you are fearful. It has been my personal experience that every decision I made out of fear or allowed fear to influence resulted in a bad decision, personal and professional. I accept that some level of fear is a healthy part of our basic Fight or Flight response, which helps us survive as a species. A healthy fear factor also prevents us from doing something dumb, like jumping out of an airplane without a parachute or hand to hand combat with a shark. But other than those two scenarios, I have found fear to be more detrimental than instrumental to the achievement of personal and corporate aspirations. I believe even the act of fleeing should be a

122

strategic or tactical decision vs. a decision made out of fear. Excuses are a product of fear – fear of failure, fear of others seeing us fail, fear of judgment, fear of not living up to expectations ... – Fear – *Fear* – **FEAR**.

If we want to find true success, we must push past the fear and move towards purposeful, strategic action.

> *"The shadow demons (fears) you've been avoiding keep you stuck in a rut, a prisoner in your own life - it's time to break free and shine!"*
> **Sharon Kirstin**

Countless times, I've observed leaders set thoughtful, purposeful, and ambitious goals, while they "prepay" their excuse for failure.

Here are a few examples of what I mean by that:

- "I will deliver revenue and profit plan this year... unless I have some really bad luck, strategic customers don't grow as planned, I lose my best sales people etc. "

- "I will lose 10 lbs. before my birthday...unless my knees start aching again and I can't work out."

- "I will attend at least half of my twins' basketball games...unless I have too much work to do."

It's easy to find solace and comfort in an excuse, especially if you have given yourself permission to fail. "I tried hard but the "world" was stacked against me." I challenge myself and every team I have led to focus on living with a No Excuses attitude. Remove excuse breeding words from your vocabulary: But, Unless, Only if, Except if, subject to…

Just make the decision to take responsibility and Own Your Power.

"I found that every single successful person I've ever spoken to had a turning point and the turning point was where they made a clear, specific, unequivocal decision that they were not going to live like this anymore. Some people make that decision at 15 and some people make it at 50 and most never make it at all."
Brian Tracy

A great foundation to No Excuse living is to stop living with your personal "Get Out of Jail Free" card. It simply means to ground yourself in a philosophy that doesn't accept making those prepaid excuses of why you can fail a task before you even start. These "prepaid" just in case excuses for failure are the sweet call of the siren's song. Remember the sirens? The mythological beings with a song so beautiful it would lure unlucky sailors to a deadly crash of their ships into the rocks. Like the siren's song, these excuses sound good, feel good, and seem logical and rational. Yet, they feed the monsters of negativity, helplessness, and incompetence. These excuses represent a significant obstacle to you realizing your full professional and personal potential as a leader.

A life filled with excuses and blaming others empowers the worst of our personality and character traits, such as anger, resentment, jealousy, hostility, dishonesty, doubt, self-loathing, and cowardice.
I know what you are thinking, "Wow Mel, that is way too much. It can't be that bad, can it?" It absolutely can. We see it every day in the people we encounter. These negative traits are contagious and have profound consequences on anyone they touch.

You know these negative people. They are "always unlucky," "always unfairly wronged," "can't get a break," "the world is against me." We can all name 5 people right now that fit this profile. When is the last time you talked with these people? How often do you connect with, hang out with, or help these people? If you were having a get together at your home, would they be at the top of your invitation list? Probably not, because no one wants to surround themselves with negativity or bring it into their homes.

124

Oh, by the way, if you keep hearing about the gang going out for drinks or talking about the great barbeque over at "Jack's" house last weekend, then it's likely a clue. The fact you are hearing about these and were not there should be a concern. You may be one of those negative people that everyone avoids.

Accepting responsibility and adopting a No Excuses mindset provides you with the best defense from joining the legion of Negative. Once you accept that you own your own power and your path to success and happiness, you don't have time in your day for all the negativity that accompany excuses and blaming.

> *"Ninety-nine percent of all failures come from people who have a habit of making excuses."*
> **George Washington Carver**

The bottom line:

- Excuses = Powerless
- No Excuses = Powerful

You did not get that promotion to a new leadership position within your organization. Instead, it went to Betty, a peer with a little less time with the company.

Powerless:

My numbers are better, so Betty only got the job because she is pretty, she knew someone in management, she is sleeping with someone, they wanted to put a woman in the role, my manager hates me, I can't get a break, this company hates me blah, blah, blah...you get the picture.

Excuses = Powerless

Powerful:

Betty, congrats on the new promotion. I look forward to working with you and hope you will let me know how I can help. Take the time to get to know Betty. You may learn something new that gave her the competitive edge. Get feedback from all the people you interviewed with and the final decision maker.

Find out:

- How can you be better?
- What could you have done differently?
- What do you need to strengthen for next time?

These options show class, maturity, and professionalism and not even a hint of pouting, anger, or resentment. Remember, No Excuses. The only person responsible for not getting the promotion is you.

No Excuses = Powerful

The scenario does not matter; you either choose to be powerful or powerless:

- You didn't get the raise or bonus you thought you deserved.
- You find out that you are making less than your peers.
- You didn't get chosen to lead or even participate in the new task force looking at pay and benefits, new structure, or potential acquisitions.
- You don't get invited to have late night drinks with your peers after a long day of meetings.

There are dozens of scenarios, but the themes remain the same.

Powerless: They don't like me, they don't respect me, I can't get a break, they don't like my race, my gender, my sexual orientation, the system is rigged against me. I will complain and wail to anyone who will listen. I will stop participating in meetings since my boss and peers don't value me. Forget late night drinks. I am tired, and they don't like me. I am going back to my room because that is where I want to be. **Powerless.**

Powerful: I must find out what my organization values most and show I am valuable and deserve the best raise and bonus. Or that my contribution is so significant that my boss makes sure I am paid at the top of my peer group because they don't want to lose me. I must figure out who can help me get onto these key task forces or projects. I need to get myself invited to late night drinks. In fact, I think next time I will just show up and hang out.

No Excuses living is a life choice. I choose powerful over powerless. I am accountable. I own it.

"The victim mindset dilutes the human potential. By not accepting personal responsibility for our circumstances, we greatly reduce our power to change them."
Steve Maraboli

Now for the kicker, and this may catch a few of you by surprise. No Excuses living makes you more likeable, happier, and content. Once you accept total responsibility for all of life's outcomes, good or bad, it is empowering beyond belief.

No Excuses Living means I am the only person responsible for my happiness and success, and no other person can give it to me or take it away.

No Excuses Living builds trust in yourself and builds people's trust in you. Accountability strengthens the bonds of trust within teams.

Powerful and Powerless Characteristics:

Accepting responsibility (Powerful)

Accepting personal responsibility is taking ownership of your behavior and the consequences of that behavior. Until you accept responsibility for your actions, it will be difficult for you to develop self-respect or the respect of others.

> *"You cannot escape the responsibility of tomorrow by evading it today."*
> **Abraham Lincoln**

Procrastination (Powerless)

Procrastination is a powerful, yet sneaky, way to have your power robbed from you. This is a way to avoid responsibility, as it delays dealing with a problem or situation long enough to allow someone else to solve it.

You can keep procrastination from making you powerless by:

- Identifying why you procrastinate. Is the task dull? Do you lack information or resources? Or is there some other cause? Once you understand why you put things off, you can try to fix the problem.

- Practice good time management, so you make time for what's important. Use tools such as Maslow's Hierarchy of Needs or Action Programs to manage your time more efficiently and effectively.

Over commitment: (Powerless)

When you take on too much, something will eventually fall through the cracks. That means you've let someone down, and most important, you've let yourself down, creating doubt, anxiety, and uncertainty, all of which work to hijack your power.

So, before you agree to a new task, think carefully about your schedule and whether you'll be able to fulfill the task to the best of your ability. If you're not sure you can sign up for the task then learn the art of saying no to the task, but yes to the person.

Honest Self-Assessment and Make Changes: (Powerful)

External accountability to your activities can open powerful learning opportunities. When something hasn't gone to plan, do an after-action review, ask for feedback, and look for ways to do things differently. This learning process will increase your power.

Reflect on your actions by spending time at the end of each day running through these two simple questions:

- What could I have done differently today?
- How can I build this change into my world tomorrow?

You are your most powerful when you are personally accountable for everything in your life. Take full ownership of what happens as a result of your choices and actions and don't blame others or make excuses.

The Consequences of Not Accepting Responsibility...A.K.A. Karma is a B@#@#!

First, not accepting responsibility has a devastating effect on respect.

There's a good chance that, when you repeatedly avoid accepting personal responsibility, someone will see and expose you. They will lose respect for you and tell other people about their experience.

"A sign of wisdom and maturity is when you come to terms with the realization that your decisions cause your rewards and consequences. You are responsible for your life, and your ultimate success depends on the choices you make."
Denis Waitley

Best Practices for Leaders to "Own your Power"

Whether you are responsible for a team or just feel responsible as a member of a team, there are strategies and tools that reinforce an "Own Your Power" mindset in your organization.

Make No Excuses
Excuses for failure, excuses about your choices in life, excuses about what you have not accomplished fuel negative and dysfunctional thinking. This negative thinking often turns into bad behaviors.

Take Responsibility for Your Life
People who take complete responsibility for their lives experience joy and empowerment, irrelevant of the circumstances. They can make choices because they understand they are responsible for the results of their choices.

You Matter
Live every day as if what you do matters, because it does. Every choice you make and every action you take matters. Your choices matter to you and create the life you live.

Thoughts Matter
"We become what we think about most." A simple quote from motivational speaker Earl Nightingale but probably one of the most apt and insightful statements I have integrated into my Own Your Power principle.

Let It Go
Even when you take control of your own life, things happen that you
130

can't control. Let go of the hurt and anger you feel and move forward.

Beware of the Power draining traps of Fate and Destiny

Are you a product of your circumstances? Has the path your life has taken been determined largely by forces beyond your control? Even if this is the case, stop believing it. Don't accept it. Convince yourself that you're in control of your life. Be in control of your life.

"In the long run, we shape our lives, and we shape ourselves. The process never ends until we die. And the choices we make are ultimately our own responsibility."
Eleanor Roosevelt

Owning Your Power is a difficult path to follow, which is why most people don't do it. It requires discipline, humility, commitment, self-awareness, and an inspired positive outlook. It is sometimes an arduous journey, but the end results and rewards are always gratifying. Bypass the path of least resistance and work to take control of your life and take responsibility for everything in your life. Think of yourself as a creator, not an acceptor. As an owner, not a victim.

No Excuses! Own Your Power!!!

No Excuses – Own Your Power
Chapter Recap

- Take responsibility for everything in your business and private life.

- Acceptance is step #1 for taking responsibility.

- Owning your power demands courage and fearlessness.

- Taking responsibility means No Excuses!

- No Excuse living – burn the boats!

- Engage in personal power building best practices.
    o Accepting responsibility – Powerful
    o Procrastination – Powerless
    o Over commitment – Powerless
    o Honest self-assessment – Powerful
    o Positive thinking – Powerful

Parker Principle #7

Embrace Humility as a Strength

"It is said that it is far more difficult to hold and maintain leadership (liberty) than it is to attain it. Success is a ruthless competitor for it flatters and nourishes our weaknesses and lulls us into complacency. We bask in the sunshine of accomplishment and lose the spirit of humility which helps us visualize all the factors which have contributed to our success. We are apt to forget that we are only one of a team, that in unity there is strength and that we are strong only as long as each unit in our organization functions with precision."
Samuel Tilden

Great leaders embrace humility. On a very basic level, it might seem that humility and great leadership can't possibly go hand-in-hand. That they are mutually exclusive characteristics.

In today's world, senior business leaders are often celebrities. Faced with their own success, press releases, interviews on cable financial shows, social media impact, and books authored, these leaders often seem larger than life. Humility is not a characteristic you typically associate with these senior leaders.

Humility, especially in the intensely competitive world of corporate politics and career progression, is often viewed by its negative synonyms, such as gentleness, submissiveness, contrition, subservience, and timidity. But with great leadership, I think we should look past the synonyms and focus closely on the definition. Humility is "the state of being humble" and being humble means "having or showing a modest or low estimate of one's self importance."

Let's do a quick exercise. Write down the top five adjectives you would like associated to you as a leader: strong, charismatic, effective, successful, intellectual, influential, respected, wise, dynamic, passionate, confident... Did I capture your five? Was humble one of your five? For 9 out of 10 leaders I posed this question to, it was not.

While no leader wants to be labelled as arrogant, few want to be known as a humble leader. It's easy to be lured into the erroneous negative assumptions associated with being a humble leader. I personally would count myself blessed if someone listed humble as one of the top 5 adjectives to describe me as a leader. It would be the ultimate compliment.

A humble leader is modest and secure enough to recognize their own weaknesses and shortcomings. They desperately seek the transparent feedback required for self-development and growth. A humble leader can subjugate their own ego and opinion to be receptive to outside ideas and assistance.

Being modest and secure means you are not afraid to seek help and guidance from others. You are willing to receive and accept others' opinions and ideas. I've talked to many leaders that were concerned this could be interpreted as a sign of weakness or as an indication of a lack of knowledge or competence. Honestly, that is a real possibility, but I think it says more about the character of the other people than that of the humble leader. A humble leader is not threatened by the valuable contribution of others; instead, they are strengthened. Humble leaders sponsor environments of open collaboration and cooperation, which drives productivity, mutual respect, and trust. This is the type of environment that attracts and retains the most talented people.

"Humility is a great quality of leadership which derives respect and not just fear or hatred."
Yousef Munayyer

Although it's never too late to integrate a level of humility into our character, it is hard work. From childhood, we are immersed in a "me first" attitude. We are also taught that winning is good, losing is bad, and sometimes, you have to be selfish, rude, and even thoughtless along the way to being a winner. Don't misinterpret the previous sentence. I am not suggesting that, as children, we are not taught, honesty, fairness, candor, and decency. But I am saying, starting at childhood, we get the repeated message that winners get what they want in life and losers get the leftovers.

I don't consider myself a naturally humble person. I am highly competitive, I love to win and hate to lose at anything. That being said, I work hard to integrate life lessons and best practices into an ever-evolving leadership paradigm grounded in humility. Sometimes, this paradigm takes me down a road less traveled, where I encounter obstacles that must be faced and overcome.

My First Existential Challenge

I was born in Fayetteville, North Carolina, and the biggest business in Fayetteville is Fort Bragg. Fayetteville is the classic "military town." It is a town built around and for the military base. Just to provide some perspective, Fayetteville has a population of about 200,000. The military population associated to Fayetteville is estimated around 53,000 active duty soldiers, 12.000 reserve soldiers, and another 63,000 family members of these soldiers.

When I was around 5 years old, my mom married an enlisted soldier, and I spent the rest of my childhood years splitting equal time on my grandmother's farm and on whatever new base my stepfather was stationed. So, I grew up around a lot of enlisted soldiers and, through that experience, developed a vision of the Army, one that painted a picture that smart, committed, and dedicated enlisted soldiers make everything work in the military.

Period.

From the most junior enlisted soldiers to the most senior non-commissioned officers, it was (and is) my belief that enlisted soldiers are the backbone of the military.

Fast forward a decade, and I headed off to the United States Military Academy. West Point, the world-renowned incubator of some of the best military officers and leaders ever produced, including Douglas MacArthur, George Patton, Dwight D. Eisenhower, and Ulysses S. Grant. The long gray line of tremendous leaders is significant. So, man, was I surprised and disappointed to learn that there was a purposeful and mandated wall between Officers and Enlisted. There were written and unwritten rules that "forbade undue familiarity between officers and enlisted."

For four years at the Academy this was taught, instilled, and ingrained into our psyche. On the one hand, there was an air of legitimacy to the concept that "familiarity breeds contempt" and that undue familiarity would "undermine command authority and thereby threaten good order, morale, or discipline in a unit." But the origins of these customs and traditions were based on class distinctions, since officers, in theory, came mostly from the "upper class."

If one thing was an absolute at the Academy, it was the sanctity of rules and traditions. I saw many interpretations of the officer and enlisted wall from professional ambivalence (this is just another rule to follow) to the extreme view that seemed to be a vision that Officers were better people than enlisted, smarter, more educated, and more socially enlightened. In other words, the real leadership of the Army.

All this was very uncomfortable for me. It went against everything I had ever learned. From my grandmother, I was ingrained with we are all equal no matter race or social status. Your social, educational, or economic circumstances doesn't make you a better person. From my military exposure, I carried the belief that enlisted soldiers were smart, committed, and dedicated. The real leaders in the Army! In fact, some of the best people I had ever known, my role models, were enlisted. While this was in direct conflict with my core beliefs, I nonetheless "accepted" it as a reality if I wanted to be an Officer in the United States Army.

> *"Pride is concerned with who is right. Humility is concerned with what is right."*
> **Ezra Taft Benson**

When I got to my first assignment as a second lieutenant in the 82nd Airborne Division as a Fire Support Officer, I found myself leading a team of awesome enlisted soldiers. I was their "LT." After a short time with the team, I made the conscious decision to diminish the customary Officer/Enlisted wall with my senior enlisted team. I made this decision understanding there was a specific army regulation (AR-600-20) that addresses all relationships between soldiers of different ranks that might cause impropriety.

In addition, "Fraternization" is a criminal Courts Martial worthy offense. Fraternization is a relationship between two soldiers having a detrimental effect on the authority of the senior. There are four required elements for the crime:

1)must be a commissioned or warrant officer
2)fraternization must be with members known to be enlisted
3)fraternization must violate the custom of the Army
4)conduct must be prejudicial to good order and discipline or bring discredit on the armed forces.

So, this decision had real existential consequences, including career destruction or, at the extreme, a criminal Courts Martial. But I bet my military career on some of the other language in that very same regulation.

1) "Our custom acknowledges that leadership and obedience are founded in sincere, deeply held emotional bonds. Leaders affectionately care for their soldiers and soldiers hold deep caring affection for their leaders. Building these emotional ties is a mark of good leadership."

2) It is difficult to predict which relationships create an adverse effect. "Many judgements are "after the fact" and are "in the eye of the professional," since they judge the results of the relationship and not the relationships themselves."

With the belief I was making the right decision for my leadership style, I decided if I had to make life or death decisions for my soldiers, I would do so treating them with the respect, comradery, and dignity that the backbone of the military deserve. I was their leader, but that did not make me their superior. So, I had them over to the house for barbeques. Got to know their wives and families. Took the time to build individual relationships as we shared many, many stories and laughs together.

You get the picture.

I listened to and integrated their suggestions. I looked to them for answers to questions I already thought I had the answer to, not just to execute my orders. We were a team, and I was the appointed team captain.

While I was on the receiving end of some negative perceptions and comments from my officer peers and "coaching" from my senior officers, I held my ground. This was my path, and it was the right path for me.

Thankfully, it worked.

During peace time, my team was one of the most effective, highly trained, top performing, and respected fire support teams in the entire

Division. Despite my senior officer coaching sessions, I continued to get Top Block ratings from them on all my performance reviews. Because, while customs and history were important, at the end of the day, results mattered.

And when I had to take this same team into combat during Operation Desert Shield/Desert Storm, guess what? In combat, nothing changed. Faced with danger and death, the team performed flawlessly, time and time again, just like we trained. They executed my orders seamlessly and without hesitation, and they knew me, how I thought, my principles and my intent, so they made the right decisions when I was not there, every single time. We were a team, and no member would let themselves fail the team.

So, my view on how leaders should engage their team members coalesced. With every promotion and new role, I led my teams the exact same way, always professional but always personal. Below are a few examples of my senior officer (LTC) ratings from my Officer Evaluation Reports.

Company Fire Support Officer:

"2LT Parker is an outstanding young officer and has distinguished himself as the best Company Fire Support Officer in the battalion. He is aggressive, tough and demanding in his training program and has produced one of the best technically and tactically proficient fire support teams in the battalion. A self-starter and demonstrated leader with outstanding potential. Promote to Captain." **2 Block Rating**

Battery Fire Direction Officer (Promotion):

"1LT Parker has demonstrated outstanding skills as Battery Fire Direction Officer. During this period, his battery deployed to the **J**oint **R**eadiness **T**raining **C**enter. 1LT Parker coordinated the complex movement of his unit which deployed by parachute, air, land and rail.

While at JRTC, his **Fire Direction Center** not only performed flawlessly under extreme hardships, they also fired a perfect live fire exercise with maneuvering infantry. The great success the FDC achieved is a direct result of 1LT Parker's exceptional technical and tactical skills as well as his natural leadership ability. Promote to Captain and following the Advanced Course, given the opportunity to command a battery." **2 Block Rating**

Battery Fire Direction Officer (Year 3):

"1LT Parker is the best Fire Direction Officer in the battalion. He implemented a rigorous training program and demonstrated this capability during a night parachute assault, when his section jumped, assembled, received a fire mission and computed firing data within ten minutes. This demanding task executed to perfection, demonstrates his ability as a trainer and a leader. His potential is unlimited. Promote to Captain and following the Advance Course, given the opportunity to command a battery." **2 Block Rating**

Battery Executive Officer (Promotion):

"1LT Parker is the best battery executive officer in the battalion. He is a hard charging young officer whose performance has been superb. His battery has the best maintenance and training program in the battalion. **He is a dynamic leader who understands soldiers and knows how to take care of them and their families.** Whether it is firing within 500 meters of maneuvering infantry or establishing new tactics and techniques at the National Training Center, 1LT Parker demonstrated the unique ability to work well under pressure and meet high standards. Mel Parker could command a battery right now! Exceptional potential, well above his peers." **1 Block Rating**

So, while my methodology of engaging my soldiers and their families was not aligned with the "norms," my results and my teams' performance in every job and at every level allowed me to follow my core and lead in the manner I knew to be "right."

My belief solidified, you can be a successful leader by being humble and earning credibility and the respect of your team vs. leading solely by the authority granted by the rank on your collar. I also learned it was possible to take the more unpopular and harder right path and still succeed, earn promotions, and be ranked above all your peers.

> *"Humility is not thinking less of yourself, it's thinking of yourself less."*
> **C. S. Lewis**

I think the final validation of the leadership lessons that I abide by today was Ranger School. If you Google US Army Ranger, you will get pages and pages of links (1.2M in 1.11s) that chronicle US Army Rangers and their long and distinguished history. The consistent theme of all this data is simply put forth in the US Army Ranger creed's second principle: *"Acknowledging the fact that a Ranger is a more elite Soldier who arrives at the cutting edge of battle by land, sea, or air, I accept the fact that as a Ranger my country expects me to move further, faster and fight harder than any other Soldier."*

Rangers are more than just physically strong. Rangers are **smart**, **tough**, **courageous**, and **disciplined**. Rangers are **self-starters**, **adventurers**, and **hard chargers.** In previous chapters, I've talked to you in detail about the challenges and hardships of attending and graduating from the US Army Ranger School. So, I won't drag you through that all again.

I want to share with you how my Ranger School experience reinforced my belief in humility as a leadership strength. It also cemented my belief that a humble leader focused on leading with credibility and mutual respect will be the most successful leader in a V.U.C.A world. My "a ha" moment so to speak.

Ranger School is one of the toughest schools in the US military. While training the most elite soldiers on the planet, with a 70% attrition rate and graduating the best leaders in the world, Ranger School requires every attendee remove all **rank** and **insignia** of authority from their uniform on Day 1. Ranger School is still the US Army, but there is no rank and its associated authority with the attendees.

A **Ranger Buddy** is simply your best friend, counselor, and sanity check. Your Ranger Buddy has your back in all circumstances. When you think you have reached the end of what you can endure, and you are on the verge of giving up, it's the voice of your Ranger Buddy that talks you back from the edge. Nobody makes it through Ranger School without a Ranger Buddy. My Ranger Buddy was a crazy Gung-Ho Recon Marine. He was also an enlisted. He reinforced my belief in everything I have known about enlisted soldiers, and I would not have my Ranger tab today without him.

> *"Selflessness is humility. Humility and freedom go hand in hand. Only a humble person can be free."*
> **Jeff Wilson**

I learned an even more important lesson that reinforced my view on leadership forever. To wear the US Army Ranger tab, you had to lead through earned respect, humility, and credibility. No rank and no enlisted vs officer wall allowed. If this works for the elite Army Rangers, then this is the way I would lead. This cemented my commitment to the leadership path that I believed was right, and I have never looked back.

Rangers Lead the Way!!!

I believe, without humility in leadership, we would walk around believing we're always right and infallible. This attitude will only distance us from others and ourselves.

"I claim to be a simple individual liable to err like any other fellow mortal. I own, however, that I have humility enough to confess my errors and to retrace my steps. "
Gandhi

Humility means being honest. When a leader can honestly reflect and evaluate their actions and behaviors, it will provide exceptional opportunities for personal and professional development.

There are real and measurable steps you can take to lead with humility. I can say, with no hesitation, they all contributed to my success in graduating Ranger School, my success as a military officer, and any success I have enjoyed in the Corporate world.

"Humility leads to strength and not to weakness. It is the highest form of self-respect to admit mistakes and to make amends for them."
John J. McCloy

Characteristics and behaviors of a humble leader:

- Admit your mistakes and share them as teachable moments.
- Engage in dialogue, not debates.
- Embrace uncertainty and ambiguity.
- Know what you don't know and be comfortable with seeking help.
- Discipline yourself to practice daily self-reflection.
- Be open and transparent.
- Cultivate Humility in Team Members, so they engage their teams as a servant leader.
- Make a sincere investment in the success of your team members.
- Embrace and promote a spirit of service.
- Don't micromanage. Trust the team members to do their job, even if it risks your failure.

- Share Authority.
- Be openly thankful for the efforts, sacrifice, and success of the team.
- Create an environment that invites feedback.
- Role model being a "good follower."
- Try to understand and meet the individual needs of team members.
- Surround yourself with a strong team.
- Be willing to own the weight of tough decisions.
- Don't allow fear to drive any decision.
- Suspend judgement and don't automatically advocate your views in your first response.
- Ask questions and be fiercely curious.

Humility inspires loyalty, helps to build and sustain cohesive, productive teamwork, and decreases staff turnover. Jim Collins was a fan of CEOs he saw demonstrating modesty and leading quietly, not charismatically. In his bestseller, *Good to Great,* he called these CEOs Level 5 executives.

Collins found Level 5 executives built enduring greatness through a paradoxical blend of personal humility and professional will.

In my career, I have found that humble leadership will:

- Build credibility and increase your ability to inspire trust, commitment, and passion.
- Reduce the chance of unwittingly responding in ways that damage morale and team engagement.
- Build relationships and an environment that results in employees wanting to share their ideas and show initiative.
- Bring out the very best in each member of the team.
- Deliver results and achieve success beyond your greatest dreams.

"Humility is the only true wisdom by which we prepare our minds for all the possible changes of life."
George Arliss

Embrace Humility as a Strength
Chapter Recap

- Great leaders embrace humility.

- A humble leader is modest and secure.

- "Humility is not thinking less of yourself, it's thinking of yourself less." – C.S. Lewis

- Humble leaders excel with the strength of their credibility and persuasion.

- Best practices of a humble leader
    o Admit mistakes.
    o Engage in more dialogue than debate.
    o Know what you don't know.
    o Openness and transparency.
    o Invest in the success of team members.
    o Don't micromanage.
    o Role model being a good follower.

Parker Principle #8

Believe in Something

"I refuse to accept the view that mankind is so tragically bound to the starless midnight of racism and war that the bright daybreak of peace and brotherhood can never become a reality... I believe that unarmed truth and unconditional love will have the final word."
Martin Luther King, Jr.

Belief is one of the most powerful catalysts to action that exists in the world today. The power of belief has put a man on the moon, eradicated slavery, secured civil rights, and been the driving force behind crusades and world wars. Powerful stuff! The only catalyst that seems to be as powerful as Belief is Fear. But beware, while these are two powerful "calls to action", the end results of those actions can be dramatically different. In my journey, I've found fear driven actions tend to be more destructive and less productive than those driven by belief.

What is belief? The statement "There are no atheists in foxholes" is an aphorism used to argue that, in times of extreme stress or fear, such as during war ("in foxholes"), all people will believe in, or hope for the assistance or intervention from a higher power (and therefore no atheists). The belief in God or a higher power is a very strong and governing belief in the world. It is a fact that the U.S. has never elected a President that did not tout some belief in God, and it is probably unlikely to change during my lifetime. While this type of higher belief is real, powerful, and critical, it is only part of the equation for leadership success. For me, my belief in God is both my foundation and the governing doctrine on how I lead.

Belief in Life:

"I believe if you keep your faith, you keep your trust, you keep the right attitude, if you're grateful, you'll see God open up new doors."
Joel Osteen

For those of you that have seen my presentation of "The Parker Principles," you would have heard me spend a decent amount of time talking about my grandmother, Augusta M Robinson, who died in late October 2016 after 98 years of a wonderful life. She was the primary source of my religious foundation. A dedicated southern Baptist, she instilled in me not only the doctrines of Christian living, but more importantly, what it means to live as a Christian. She believed this is not something you turn on for church Sunday mornings then act and live differently the other 6 days of the week. I adopted from her the philosophy that living as a Christian is a 360-degree life view that should also govern how you interact with people and how you lead.

Principles like: integrity, treat all people equally with respect, treat people how you would like to be treated, help those in need, see the good in people first, optimism, and self-belief have governed all aspects of my life. I recognize that I'm flawed and have made many mistakes in life. I subscribe to the belief that, if you live, you will make mistakes. I was also taught to own those mistakes, learn from them, and be a better person on the other side. Whether in life, leadership, or business, those principles have been deeply relevant to any success I have been blessed to achieve.

Belief in Leadership:

"Don't underestimate the power of your vision to change the world. Whether that world is your office, your community, an industry or a global movement, you need to have a core belief that what you contribute can fundamentally change the paradigm or way of thinking about problems."
Leroy Hood

In corporate America, every day that you lead, you are writing and telling your story. This story will be greatly influenced by Belief...*or, even more specifically, by faith.*

Regardless of your spiritual beliefs, your leadership legacy will be greatly defined by your faith. This *faith* does not necessarily relate to going to a place of worship or engaging in religious rituals. This faith is simply the catalyst and the construct to act on what we believe is right, true, and just as a leader.

When leaders act, they get results. When they act with belief and faith, they get lasting results that resonate and contribute long after they're gone. This is the type of leadership that makes a difference. What we believe to be true, the principles of our faith, and the resilience to stand for what is right and just will help you write the most amazing leadership story possible.

"Your leadership legacy will be determined by your faith."
Bill Blankschaen

Belief in Business:

"A passionate belief in your business and personal objectives can make all the difference between success and failure. If you aren't proud of what you're doing, why should anybody else be?"
Richard Branson

For the leader of a business, belief and faith can be the critical difference between tremendous success and cataclysmic failure. These items are at the core of who we are, why we do what we do, our approach to change, how we handle a crisis situation, and how we lead.

Your belief may or may not be true, logical, or even rational, but your belief is at the heart of unlocking the potential in any organization and making your leadership style work to achieve the desired results.

Great leaders know the first critical step to changing people's behavior is to understand their perspectives and embrace their desires and beliefs.

I'm a strong believer in action. The foundational quotation for my entire leadership career:

"Leadership is Action, Not Position."

This great quote comes from Donald H. McGannon, who ran the Westinghouse Broadcasting Corporation and served as President of the National Urban League.

While you can be put into a position of leadership by rank, hierarchy, or title, this is not the same as being appreciated and respected as "the leader "or "our leader." You can't just declare yourself "the leader"; you must earn that title. By default, to be "the leader", you must have willing and committed followers.

150

People follow people, not positions. They respect people whom they trust. They tag along with people in whom they believe. They follow people who have demonstrated through their actions that they deserve to be followed.

These actions require no certain "position." The actions you take need to inspire people to trust and follow you. You can't "fake it until you make it" or just talk about it. If a leader does not act, nothing happens. It has been my experience that leadership action will only happen if you have belief and faith, in yourself and in the actions you plan to take.

I will address the power of self-belief a little later. But for now, let's talk about the belief and faith in the actions you plan to take. If you don't believe in your own course of action and decisions, no one else will. Action and beliefs, beliefs and action are interdependent.

"Your work is going to fill a large part of your life, and the only way to be truly satisfied is to do what you believe is great work. And the only way to do great work is to love what you do. If you haven't found it yet, keep looking. Don't settle. As with all matters of the heart, you'll know when you find it."
Steve Jobs

A leader must convince others that the course of action they are proposing is the right one. That the decisions and strategies they are employing are the right ones. In almost every situation, but especially situations where change and transformation are required to succeed, a leader must evolve and escalate "their game." This is about going beyond decisions that are logical and goals that are SMART to moving towards a vision of the future that aligns with your internal belief system.

I am an avid proponent and practitioner of strengths-based leadership

151

(Tom Rath and Barry Conchie). One of the foundational principles in their book, *Strengths based Leadership,* is that to lead from your strengths, you must know, accept, and understand your strengths. Also, after many years of practical use, I have found Clifton's *Strength Finder* to be an essential tool for helping leaders build on their strengths and the strengths of the people they lead.

Clifton identifies 34 different leadership strengths or themes, and one those themes is **Belief.** Leaders strong in the **Belief** theme have certain core values that are unchanging. Out of these values emerge a defined purpose for their life. In most cases, your **Belief** theme causes you to be family-oriented, altruistic, even spiritual, and to value responsibility and high ethics, both in yourself and others. If **Belief** is one of your strengths, acting within the guidelines of these core values gives your life meaning and satisfaction. From your viewpoint, success is more than money and prestige. These core values of **Belief** provide you with direction, guiding you through temptations and distractions, toward a consistent set of priorities and actions. Your **Belief** makes you easy to trust. People will follow leaders they trust.

"One life is all we have and we live it as we believe in living it. But to sacrifice what you are and to live without belief, that is a fate more terrible than dying."
Joan of Arc

In my career, my Belief system has defined my leadership paradigm. My Belief:

- Gives me clarity of mission.

"It's not hard to make decisions when you know what your values are."
Roy Disney

- Demands I act with integrity in all circumstances. The West

Point motto - Duty, Honor, and Country were more than just words. They are the three pillars that substantiate all aspects of my Character.

"We have to stand up for what we believe in, even when we might not be popular for it. Honesty starts with being ourselves, authentic and true to who we are and what we believe in, and that may not always be popular, but it will always let you follow your dreams and your heart."
Tabatha Coffey

- Keeps me grounded and never lets me forget my humble beginnings on a pig and tobacco farm in North Carolina.

"When someone shows you who they are, believe them the first time."
Maya Angelou

- Helps me provide the vision, coaching, and guidance owed my teams.

"At the end of the day, people follow those who know where they're going."
Jack Trout

- Allows me to act courageously even when facing the toughest situations.

"Human spirit is the ability to face the uncertainty of the future with curiosity and optimism. It is the belief that problems can be solved, differences resolved. It is a type of confidence. And it is fragile. It can be blackened by fear and superstition."
Bernard Beckett

- Allows me to fail with dignity, pick myself up and get back on mission.

"I believe that God has put gifts and talents and ability on the inside of every one of us. When you develop that and you believe in yourself and you believe that you're a person of influence and a person of purpose, I believe you can rise up out of any situation."
Joel Osteen

- Informs me that every problem has a solution (although sometimes an unpleasant solution) and every dream (no matter how improbable) is achievable.

"You must never confuse faith that you will prevail in the end–which you can never afford to lose–with the discipline to confront the most brutal facts of your current reality."
Admiral Stockdale

Self-Belief:

I want to take a little time to talk about the power of Self-Belief. I am not talking about arrogance, boastfulness, or an inflated ego but a self-belief that translates into self-confidence and a winning attitude (swagger). Self-belief is the knowledge you have within you the resources, talent, and resilience to overcome obstacles and to keep the momentum going until you have completed the task.

"If you believe in yourself and have dedication and pride - and never quit, you'll be a winner. The price of victory is high but so are the rewards."
Paul Bryant

Throughout my career, my very best performance as a leader has been with organizations that needed a turnaround or transformation. While these are the business situations in which I thrive as a leader, they are intense, stressful, and emotionally tough. I have built my career on a reputation of being able to wade into the toughest business situations and come out on the other side with an inspired and winning team, running a growing and more profitable business.

I think we all would find it hard to bet our career or our family's welfare on a leader that was unsure, ambivalent, or lacked confidence in their skills, abilities, strategies, or decisions. All leaders are human and have "moments" of uncertainty and doubt. In these moments, I count on the external and internal powers of retrospection and introspection to get me back on track.

- Retrospection (external) is the act of looking back on and reviewing past events or situations.

- Introspection (internal) is the examination or observation of one's own mental and emotional processes.

"Don't let fear or insecurity stop you from trying new things. Believe in yourself. Do what you love. And most importantly, be kind to others, even if you don't like them."
Stacy London

As I look back over my career from my first leadership role in the military to every subsequent job, I have one consistent tagline I use to sign off on my emails and correspondence - **Keep the Faith!** I am not sure of the exact moment this became my "battle cry", but I see now that some instinct was revealing to me the significance and importance of Belief for all stakeholders to any leader's success.

Why is Self-Belief so important? You can't ask anyone to believe in you or **"Keep the Faith"** in your leadership, decisions, and strategy, unless you actually believe in it yourself. Self-Belief inspires us to try, and it motivates us to keep going under the most arduous circumstances.

"If you really believe in what you're doing, work hard, take nothing personally and if something blocks one route, find another. Never give up."

155

It has been proven time after time throughout history how the rock-hard faith and belief held by one individual can have a powerful impact on the behavior of many people.

The same principle applies to leadership and companies facing a financial turnaround or a difficult business environment. The faith and belief held by the leader in the strategy, the brand, the products, and the people must be rock solid. This faith allows the leader to act and lead in a way that captures and unlocks the talent, loyalty, and heart of teams.

As a "turnaround leader", staff reductions, right-sizing the organization, budget cutbacks, and cost containment are an uncomfortable reality. To maintain profitability, action must be taken. These are the times a leader must look in the mirror and ask...

- Do I have the faith?
- Do I have self-belief?

Because, if faith and belief are not there, then it will be difficult, if not impossible, to engage and convince others of the necessity and the rewards of the turnaround. Your people must have faith and belief in you to face the difficult challenges of business.

"Your belief determines your action and your action determines your results, but first you have to believe."
Mark Victor Hansen

Believe in Something
Chapter Recap

- Belief is one of the most powerful catalysts to action that exists in the world.

- Belief in life and Belief in leadership are an unstoppable combination.

- For a great leader, belief and faith can be the critical difference between tremendous success and cataclysmic failure.

- The only way to change an organization's behavior is to change their belief.

- Leaders that have strength in belief possess core values that are unchanging and predictable. This predictability inspires trust by followers.

- Strong belief provides a leader with:
    o Clarity of mission
    o Character and Integrity
    o Vision
    o Courage

- Self-Belief translates into self-confidence, resiliency, and a winning attitude.

Parker Principle #9

"Physical fitness is not only one of the most important keys to a healthy body, it is the basis of dynamic and creative intellectual activity."
John F. Kennedy

Now, this Parker Principle has probably been my most debated and challenged leadership principle. This is for many reasons. On the surface, it looks like the least controllable and most subjective of all the principles. It hits the edges of items that make most of us uncomfortable in the corporate environment – appearance, fitness, visual conveyance, what do I look like to others etc.

Yes, it matters how you look. Yes. it matters how you sound. Yes, it matters how you sit, stand, and present. Yes, Yes, Yes!

I assume you are reading my book because you have talent, ambition, and potential. You strive for the challenge and rewards of senior leadership. So, you should demand and value transparency and reality above all else. I recognize this flies in the face of the core belief that, if you are talented, work hard, and deliver results, you will be given a chance to lead and advance to senior leadership positions. That is a system that sounds fair and just, but that's not the reality you will face in the corporate world. You need more.

My adult life has been dedicated to mastering the craft and unlocking the potential of Leadership. I am a lifetime student of Leadership and have started to hyper focus on the mission of sharing the learnings, stumbles, rewards, and joy of that journey.

So, let's have some straight talk. I like to use metaphors, so forgive me for the journey into racing. Imagine yourself as a race car. While there are many types of racing, for our journey, we will focus on the two most popular:

- Formula car (FORMULA ONE)
- Stock car (NASCAR)

For the sake of our journey, you are either a Formula One race car or a NASCAR racecar.

A **Formula One race car** is a single-seat, open cockpit, open wheel racing car with substantial front and rear wings and an engine positioned behind the driver. Formula One cars race at speeds of up to 240 mph with V10 engines producing between 980 and 1,000 HP.

A **NASCAR race car** is a closed cockpit, closed wheel race car with minimal front and rear wings, and an engine positioned in front of the driver. NASCAR cars race at speeds up to 200 mph with V8 engines producing between 860-900 HP.

Formula One racing started in Europe, and it was considered the racing of royalty. **NASCAR** racing originated in the southern US, where "good old boys" were running moonshine with modified supped up every day cars direct off the manufacturing assembly line. (Side note. This is where the term stock car comes from.) It was considered the racing of the common people.

So, in my seminars or coaching sessions, when I ask people the question, which type of race car do you want to be? The quick answer, 90% of the time is "a Formula One car, of course!" These cars are sexier, faster, and more powerful. They are literally the more agile race car of the elite. I usually stop them right there and suggest the right response should have been to ask the clarifying question of what type of race will it be?

That answer will truly help determine what type of car is needed.

Formula One cars are the fastest road course racing cars in the world. Racing around a 3 to 4-mile public road track with left and right turns, the course requires very high cornering speeds and a high level of skill. Light, sleek with masterful aerodynamic design, these cars are engineering masterpieces.

NASCAR cars race on predominantly oval 1 to 2-mile tracks with 3 to 4 left turns. These cars have minimal aerodynamic design and are much heavier and durable than Formula One cars.

I don't want to be a sexy, sleek, and light Formula One car in a NASCAR race, where the acceptable jostling, bumping, and pushing would be catastrophic to the less durable and lighter Formula One car. The understanding of what type of race you are in is basically understanding what type of organizational culture you are in. This initial determination of your culture will directly determine your success or failure at that organization.

Now, don't miss this! This is an important point...huge really. It's not really a quick hitting Parker Principle, but it is so important that I am planning to write a book specifically on Culture: Diagnose, Survive and Thrive!

So back on message. In contrast with most forms of racing, minor car-to-car contact is generally accepted in a NASCAR race. This may happen in the form of forcing another vehicle out of the way or pushing a competing vehicle forward for mutual benefit. NASCAR cars are generally built to be tolerant of superficial damage to bodywork, whereas the Formula One cars can experience severe operational issues with even the slightest spoiler damage. So, no matter how powerful and agile the Formula One car may be, it is unlikely to help you win a NASCAR race and vice versa.

You have to be the right race car for the race you are trying to win. Once that informed decision is made, you now must be the most powerful, fastest, toughest, and most agile car in the race. Notwithstanding the force of luck, both good and bad, usually the fittest car with the best driver has the best chance of winning any race. The car and the driver are one machine, completely codependent on each other. The fittest car with a bad driver usually has no chance of winning. This is equally true with the best driver on the track being forced to race in an unfit car.

In this metaphor, the race car is your body, and the driver is your brain. To unlock your career potential, the total machine must function at maximum performance. The fact remains that no matter how intelligent you are, you have to have a fit car to win.

This is usually when the first hands start to shoot up. Well, what do you mean by fit? Great question, when I am talking about the "Be Fit" in this Parker Principle.

It is **NOT**:

- Your Weight
- Your BMR (Body Mass Ratio)
- Your ability to bench press 300lbs
- Your ability to run a 5-minute mile
- A size 2 or a 32-inch waist

It **IS** about

- How you feel about what you see in the full-length mirror before you get dressed in the morning
- Being healthy
- Feeling strong and energized for the day ahead
- Having high energy and engagement at 6AM and 6PM

- How you manage stress and turmoil
- The image of confidence and strength you portray to the world

It has been my experience that a fit leader is usually a better leader for a multitude of reasons. If you know my body of work in leadership, then you know how much my becoming an Army Ranger shaped my view on leadership and how I lead. There is probably no tougher leadership school on the planet than the Army Ranger School. Graduating from Ranger School is one of the proudest most impactful moments of my life. It marked a turning point of successfully overcoming so many fears that inhibited and detracted from my ability to be a great leader. I regularly wear my Ranger lapel pin as a constant reminder of not only the growth, toughness, fearlessness, and perseverance I needed to obtain it, but also of the character, qualities, and type of leader I strive to be every day.

As an Army Ranger, you take the Ranger Creed seriously. The R.A.N.G.E.R. creed is the official mission statement of the U.S. Army Rangers, consisting of six hard wired tenets for Rangers to live by, one for each letter in the word RANGER. I have internalized the RANGER creed, and it is an embedded and integrated part of how I try to live and lead. There is a copy of the entire RANGER creed at the beginning of this book, but for the purpose of this Parker Principle, and the interconnection of fitness and leadership I will call your attention to three of the six tenets A, N and R

Acknowledging the fact that a Ranger is a more elite Soldier, who arrives at the cutting edge of the battlefield by land, sea, or air. I accept the fact that *as a Ranger my country expects me to move further, faster and fight harder than any other Soldier*

Never shall I fail my comrades. *I will always keep myself mentally alert, physically strong and morally straight and I will shoulder more than my fair share of the task whatever it may be, one hundred percent and then some.*

Readily will I display the ***intestinal fortitude*** required to fight on to the Ranger objective and complete the mission though I be the lone survivor.

It is not an accident that three of the six Ranger tenets tie fitness to leadership. So how does this apply to the need and competitive advantage of being fit in civilian leadership? Being fit brings a multitude of strengths, but by far, the most impactful is Confidence.

Confidence:

Being fit will make you more confident, both self-confident and the external perception of confidence. Confidence is a critical component of a leader's ability to lead. It is the cornerstone or foundation for successful leadership. You can teach a leader many skills: accountability, coaching, strategic thinking, problem solving, decision-making, effective communication…truly the list goes on and on. Yet, a leader with these skills but lacking confidence will find it difficult to get people to follow them.

If you don't have the self-confidence in your skills and abilities to accomplish the mission, no one else will either. The good news is there is a natural level of trust given to new leaders confident in their abilities to get the job done, even before they have proven themselves. I have found that confidence driven trust becomes naturally associated with competence. Now, to maintain that trust, you must be competent and deliver results. However, it is that initial vote of internal confidence that provides you with your first opportunity to be competent. Great leaders have confidence in the strength of their vision, the impact of their communication, their courage to make tough decisions, and their ability to accomplish the mission. Confident leaders embrace change, take risks, are calm under pressure, own mistakes, and are open to feedback from any source.

"In my judgment, physical fitness is basic to all forms of excellence and to a strong, confident nation."
Robert Kennedy

Confidence is also critical in a leader's ability to get noticed. One of my core teachings is that being fit is not dictated by your size, body shape, or BMI (Body Mass Index). Being fit is about being strong and feeling strong. That builds confidence. A great example comes to mind. At one organization where I worked as a general manager, I conducted monthly half day sales and marketing meetings where we were always looking at new ideas and creative ways to serve the customer and beat the competition.

After many months of this meeting, I noticed a young lady that presented nothing new and never contributed to the overall discussion. Now, as a general manager, my initial thought was why am I paying this young lady to sit in a meeting and not contribute? In my mind, the best decision for my boss and shareholders is to let her go and replace her with someone that could add value to the meeting and discussion. If I am using shareholder money to pay your salary, you had better be contributing to shareholder value.

So, I watched for a few more meetings then decided it just was not one bad day or one bad meeting; this young lady was not a contributing force on the team. I concluded it may be time to make a change. What I've learned over my career is to ensure a decision of this magnitude is made with maximum information and at a personal level, so I set up a one on one with this young lady to validate my assessment and feel comfortable that letting her go was the best decision for the business.

What I found during our one on one was that my assessment was horribly wrong. When we sat down for our one on one, I found, not only was she incredibly intelligent, but she was incredibly creative and innovative. She shared with me thoughts and ideas that were basically...brilliant. As a leader, I am also a believer in transparent conversations with my people, so I let her know why she was there and the assessment I had of her from almost 6 months of observation. I noted what we discussed in the last hour had been better than most of the ideas presented by her teammates for the last six months, so why had she been so silent and non-impactful in the sales and marketing meetings? At that moment, I had one of my Be Fit "aha moments." As a matter of custom at these meetings, when you are selling your ideas, you get up and present your ideas standing in front of an audience of 15 to 20 people.

What I discovered or noticed for the first time is this young lady was not, as we say, slim and did not possess a Hollywood model body style. This young lady was too embarrassed by her body to get up in front of a crowd of people and present. She was experiencing complete lack of confidence.

My coaching moment to her was to forget about her body shape, get fit, feel strong, and she will gain confidence in that strength. As brilliant as you are (race car driver), you had no confidence in the fitness of your racecar (body), so it almost cost you the whole race (job). Then we made a commitment to each other. I committed to be patient in her building confidence and contributing to the meetings, and she committed to being fit. There was tremendous determination and ambition in this young lady. During this transition time, I still needed her brilliance, so I built in a monthly one on one to get her ideas, views, and opinions so the organization received her value as she worked on building her confidence.

As she got more fit, she became more confident and she participated more in the meetings. Every meeting was an improvement on the prior and soon the need for my "back channel" one on ones ended, and she was now a major contributor during every interaction. In fact, within a very short time, I promoted her and she started leading a small team of marketers. This young lady went from almost being fired to a leadership promotion, not because of more education or more brilliance

(She already had those!), but because of more confidence. Be fit, Be Strong, Be confident.

"I've always believed fitness is an entry point to help you build that happier, healthier life. When your health is strong, you're capable of taking risks. You'll feel more confident to ask for the promotion. You'll have more energy to be a better mom. You'll feel more deserving of love."
Jillian Michaels

Other Be Fit Benefits:

Energy

Being fit will give you more energy throughout the day. A leader is expected to be as engaged and alert at 6PM as they are at 6AM. Being a leader means you are always "ON", and you need a high and consistent energy level to do so effectively. A leader with more energy is likely to face the obstacles and challenges of the day with more alertness, vigor, creativity, and productivity.

Influence

Being fit maximizes your ability to influence, and the ability to influence maximizes your ability to lead. Influence is the ability to affect a person's emotions, opinions, or behaviors and is the very essence of leadership. It is human nature or genetic programming for groups of people. (i.e. your team) to be influenced by confidence and strength, the very essence of being fit.

Toughness

Being fit enables you to face challenges and overcome obstacles with energy and focus. As a leader, you will be presented with a myriad of challenges and obstacles every day. To be fit, it takes discipline, focus, and mental toughness. Those same three qualities will make you a better leader.

Stress

Being fit is one of the best ways to handle stress. I'm sure that there is an abundance medical data behind this theory. The release of endorphins that make us feel good and the value of the distraction that exercise provides from daily anxiety are just two examples. Whether you take my experience or you find out about the science of fitness, being fit is a great way to manage the stresses of leadership.

Self–Discipline

I have found that, 99% of the time, to be fit, you must have self-discipline. Self-discipline allows a leader to set the right example and model the right behavior all the time. Remember, a leader is always "ON", not just at the office or during work hours. The self-discipline required to be fit by sticking to a workout plan and diet is the same self-discipline a leader must have to lead.

> *"Movement is a medicine for creating change in a person's physical, emotional, and mental states."*
> **Carol Welch**

Mental Alertness

One lesson of success I learned in Ranger school is that, as a leader, at the end of a 12-mile road march, you must have the stamina and mental alertness to still make good decisions. Fatigue is not an acceptable excuse for a leader to make a bad decision, yet I have seen fatigue time and time again cause even good leaders to do just that. Being fit is the best defense against a fatigue related bad decision.

Organizational Health

168

As a general manager, one of my most significant non-customer facing costs that impact P&L is healthcare. The physical health of your organization is a competitive advantage in any market place. As a leader, it is your job to set the example or, more important, lead by example. It is difficult to ask the people that follow you to be healthy and fit if you are not modeling the same behavior. As a leader in business, you maximize potential and results when you have a happy, healthy, and energized team.

Relationships

We live in a world where relationships matter. It is my experience that being fit helps you build better relationships. Being fit often makes you more confident, approachable, and sociable. Being fit makes you feel good about yourself and that often translates to you laughing more and treating others better. The overall positive energy translates into better relationships.

"I feel if I'm healthy and happy, I look good. With a good mixture of fitness and healthy food I always feel great!"
Candice Swanepoel

Your Personal Brand

As the adage goes, "True leaders lead from the front." Your personal brand is directly connected to your ability to lead with success. As you have noticed, my personal brand is basically the Mel model of the Ranger Creed. Rangers are strong and tough, cool under fire, take care of their people, lead through credibility, and always accomplish the mission.

What is your personal brand?

Without a strong personal brand, you will find it very difficult to build trust, belief, and confidence in your leadership. Being fit must be a part of every leader's personal brand.

> *"Take care of your body. It's the only place you have to live."*
> **Jim Rohn**

Rangers Lead the Way!

Be Fit, Strong and Confident
Chapter Recap

- Great leadership requires fitness of mind, body, and spirit.

- Being fit is more about how you feel about yourself than how you look in a mirror.

- Fitness of mind, body, and spirit expands a leaders' confidence.

- Benefits of being a fit, strong, and confident leader.
  o Energy
  o Influence
  o Toughness
  o Stress management
  o Self-discipline
  o Mental Alertness
  o Organizational health
  o Stronger relationships
  o Your personal brand

Parker Principle # 10

Be Enthusiastic and Optimistic

Enthusiasm and Optimism are contagious!

Enthusiasm is strong excitement about something, a strong feeling of active interest in something you like or enjoy and something causing a feeling of excitement and active interest.

> *"Every memorable act in the history of the world is a triumph of enthusiasm. Nothing great was ever achieved without it because it gives any challenge or any occupation, no matter how frightening or difficult, a new meaning. Without enthusiasm you are doomed to a life of mediocrity but with it you can accomplish miracles."*
> **Og Mandino**

Optimism is an attitude originally derived from the Latin *optimum*, meaning "best." It is a doctrine that this world is the best possible world, an inclination to put the most favorable construction upon actions and events or to anticipate the best possible outcome.

> *"I am fundamentally an optimist. Whether that comes from nature or nurture, I cannot say. Part of being optimistic is keeping one's head pointed toward the sun, one's feet moving forward. There were many dark moments when my faith in humanity was sorely tested, but I would not and could not give myself up to despair. That way lays defeat and death."*
> **Nelson Mandela**

Enthusiasm and optimism are a dynamic duo, mutually supportive with each fueling the other. One without the other diminishes outcomes, whereas together, they maximize potential and deliver extraordinary results.

If you doubt the absolute power of the Enthusiasm and Optimism (E&O) combination, just take a moment to consider the debilitating and destructive effects of their inverse combination of Apathy and Pessimism. There is no worse combination of characteristics for any leader: low energy and disheartened. You can be guaranteed as a leader that you will face business and leadership obstacles, conflicts, and emergencies that must be overcome. But the pessimistic leader will not only fear the worst, but they will spread their fear and dismal outlook to their organization, which will prevent that organization from performing at its best.

The optimistic leader can keep going, despite the hurdles that might be facing the organization. These leaders understand the inspiring and contagious power of their positive outlook and that the people they lead look to them for direction and energy. The optimistic leader emanates a force of resiliency and a long-term perspective that provides the stability that tends to decrease chaos, stress, and anxiety within the workforce.

Now, let's not confuse optimism with a Pollyannaish perspective. I am an eternal optimist. I believe in the best of any situation and of people until I learn something different. I like to call my leadership style of optimism, Informed Optimism.

Let's dive a little deeper into ***Informed Optimism*** and its place as a Leadership Force Multiplier. As you have seen throughout this book, my experience as a US Army Ranger has had a tremendous impact in shaping my leadership style and principles. I consistently reference items from the RANGER Creed as foundational aspects of great leadership. Reference the total RANGER creed in the introduction. For this story, let's focus on the A and R points of the creed.

Acknowledging the fact that a Ranger is a more elite Soldier who arrives at the cutting edge of battle by land, sea, or air. I accept the fact that as a Ranger my country expects me to move further, faster and fight harder than any other Soldier.

Readily will I display the intestinal fortitude required to fight on to the Ranger objective and complete the mission though I be the lone survivor.

So, how do these Ranger tenets tie on to the Parker Principle of Enthusiasm and Optimism and, more specifically, to the power of Informed E&O?

During my military days as a Field Artillery officer in the 82nd Airborne Division, we were conducting a training road march. This was basically a timed 6-mile road march, with each soldier carrying their weapon and a rucksack (Army back pack) weighing between 30 and 40lbs. As a matter of clarity, unlike the infantry, the field artillery rarely marches or walks with their cannons anywhere. Either the artillery piece is pulled by a vehicle or is self-propelled. So, field artillery soldiers are not used to any forced road marches and struggle to complete.

Now, fast forward 2 or 3 miles into the march. I started to see a slowdown of the entire group; some soldiers were dragging their feet, with expressions on their faces that clearly indicated surrender was imminent. As I looked down the line, I could see quite a few were starting to fall behind the main group. Just for the record, if a leader doesn't get everyone across the finish line in the prescribed time, then the whole unit gets a FAIL. It is all or nothing. I am the leader, so I am responsible and accountable for the performance of my unit. It seemed like failure was imminent. So, what do I do now?

In that instance, I think instinct kicked in. Without even thinking about it, I knew it was time to bring out **Ranger Mel** to try to salvage the situation. So, I run up and down the long single file line of about 100 soldiers shouting, cheering, encouraging the team. I was running and jumping around like an insane person, and the looks I initially received validated that everyone thought I was having a heat stroke or had lost my mind. For the folks falling behind, I ran all the way back to the end of the line (Now remember, I am also in full gear and carrying a radio, so I am carrying at least 50lbs of equipment!). When I get to the last person in the line, I grab the 40lb rucksack off their back, put it on mine, and then start running back up to the front, encouraging that individual to run with me. And they do.

Once I got them close to the front of the line, I gave them back their rucksack and told them, "Now all you have to do is keep up with the person in front of you! You've got this!" I then took off and ran back again to the end of the line, shouting and encouraging the team as I passed by for them to keep pushing hard and catch up to the soldier in front of them. Can you guess what happened when I made it to the end? Yep, I grabbed another rucksack and off we went.

Rinse and repeat. I worked through this cycle maybe another 5 to 6 times over the final 3 or 4 miles until we finished. As we approached the finish line, I ran along the line back to the front, encouraging everyone I passed to push hard to the finish. I finally get to the front just in time to be the first one across the finish line. I was taught leaders lead from the front and by example. After I crossed the finish line, I immediately turned around still in full gear and greeted every soldier with a high five and words of praise as they crossed.

Now you may think, great story, but wait! There is more! An amazing transformation happened right before my eyes, one that even surprised me. As I was greeting each soldier, I looked out and noticed the soldiers were picking up speed, some even running toward me standing at the finish line. Amazing. And that's not all. I also saw some soldiers come alongside another soldier that was struggling, grab them by the shoulder or arm, and they picked up speed toward me as a team, each one inspiring and encouraging the other. It was a fantastic sight and a proud moment that helped define my view on leadership and the belief that every team deserves to be led by an enthusiastic and optimistic leader.

An additional risk of these timed marches is the rule that the evaluated time does not stop until the last soldier crosses the finish line. The march is a mission that requires massive individual effort on the part of each soldier, but you can only succeed as a team. You either Pass or Fail based on the team time. Just like in business, you win and lose as a team. To succeed, massive individual efforts, across multiple functions, must come together to deliver one profit number.

This march was a significant "aha" moment for me. The joy and pride of the team accomplishment and the incredible individual efforts and teamwork I observed were moving. But I now had a new understanding of the power that Informed Enthusiasm and Optimism add to a leader as a Force Multiplier. So, I will share a secret with you and only you. My unit was amazed, awed, and inspired by the "super human" effort of Ranger Mel during that march. But that effort of enthusiasm and optimism also carried significant risk. Remember, I was running around carrying my own 50lb load. And, when I would run shouting and yelling to the back of the line and grab the last straggler's backpack, I was carrying 80 to 90lbs of equipment. Then I would make that soldier run with me and not only catch up to the unit but keep running up to the front part of the line, give them their rucksack back, then off I went running to go get the next straggler. All sounds wonderful, right?

Let's look at some possible leader failure "what if" scenarios. **What if** the first time I ran to the back to grab a straggler, instead of running with them to the front of the line, I run out of juice? I can't make it back to the front, and in fact, I have now burnt so much energy trying to carry two rucksacks that I start to fade, fall back, and I become the straggler. **What if** that happened on the first round-trip or even the sixth round-trip to the back? In either case, as the leader, running out of gas means not only do I not end the march in the front as the first person to cross the finish line, but now I am at the back. I am the one bringing up the rear, and every one of my soldiers has to turn around and observe their leader, a man they must trust with their lives and well-being, dragging and struggling just to make it through. Instead of an asset, I would become a liability.

This would be an absolute leadership disaster, no matter how many successful trips I made to the back. No matter how much enthusiasm and optimism I showed, if I cannot finish the job, then I become a liability. No matter how honorable my intentions were, if I crossed the finish line in the back, the loss of leadership credibility would have been catastrophic and possibly unrecoverable. So now, the Ranger Mel efforts may not seem so smart.

Why did I risk a potential leadership disaster to go into the Ranger Mel mode? Informed Enthusiasm and Optimism.

Here is the secret.

Rangers are not "super human"; they just seem to be because of their knowledge and experience. You may have heard me talk about my time at Ranger School. It was literally the toughest few months of my entire life. I thought I was in maximum physical condition when I arrived, but by the end at graduation day, I had lost over 40lbs. When I show my friends a picture of our graduation class, they have trouble identifying me in the picture because of the severe physical change that occurred.

In my view, one of the primary goals of Ranger School is to take you to the very limits of your mental, physical, and spiritual capabilities. While you are undergoing tremendous amounts of physical and mental stress, starvation, sleep deprivation, injuries etc., you are also being encouraged every day to quit. Remember, they call it LOM or Lack of Motivation. And, once you LOM out of Ranger School, you can never, ever return.

178

Let's take a quick look at the E tenant on the Ranger Creed:

*Energetically will I meet the enemies of my country. I shall defeat them on the field of battle for I am better trained and **will fight with all my might. Surrender is not a Ranger word.** I will never leave a fallen comrade to fall into the hands of the enemy and under no circumstances will I ever embarrass my country.*

I will fight with all my might. Surrender (or quitting) is not a Ranger word. The Ranger Instructors (RI's) are famous for getting into your head at your absolute lowest moment and convincing you to LOM. To be transparent, everyone, and I mean everyone that attends Ranger School, will come close to quitting at some point during the course. It is just human nature when you are suffering; you just want it to end.

I also had my moment. I remember one cold wintery night in the mountains of Dahlonega, Georgia; after a forced river crossing in water up to our necks, we then had to set a patrol base in the woods, no heat no fire, nothing. I am laying on the ground, weapon at the ready, covering my sector of fire. My body is shaking uncontrollably, and my teeth are chattering like a machine gun. I literally believed I would get hypothermia and die, right there on the cold ground. I am at my lowest point, and a RI comes up to me and starts his whisper campaign.

"You look really cold, Ranger Parker. I read your file. You are a West point grad, in the 82nd Airborne Division and in the Field Artillery. You don't really need this piece of cloth "Ranger tab" on your shoulder. Your family is back home waiting on you. You have everything to live for. You are already a badass. You don't need a little piece of cloth to justify yourself. You don't want to die out here in the woods. Just say the word, and I will get you out of here, and you will have heat and a cup of hot coffee in your hands within an hour. Just say the word."

It felt like he spent hours on his whisper campaign. Don't believe for a second I did not consider taking his offer. I remember thinking, "Yeah, he is right. I don't need this shit. I don't need this torture. This is

179

bullshit! He is right. I have everything to live for, family, good career etc. etc." On and on, my mind was breaking down my will. "He is right. I am out of here!!! Wait! What???"

I was in the throes of a major internal battle, and I was losing. Two things saved me:

1) My Recon Marine Ranger Buddy lying beside me telling me to ignore the RI and hold on
2) All of a sudden, over the chatter of my teeth, I could hear other ranger candidates being evacuated back to the camp to "get their hot coffee."

This whisper campaign was not just me. RI's were all over the patrol base making these offers to various members of the patrol. We lost 15 people that night, LOM. I learned a very valuable lesson that night. I found that I could take a huge amount of physical pain and discomfort and still do my job without quitting if I was able to win the battle in my own mind.

I never came close to quitting again over the next two months of torture, no matter how bad the situation. Each day after the river crossing, I broke through the old and established a new "limit" on the amount of suffering and misery I could handle. So, at that point, anything less than my new limits was a piece of cake.

This is what happened on that road march. First, forgive me if I don't get the exact numbers correct. As with many war stories, the farther you get away from the actual event, the bigger the story becomes in your memory. We had forced marches in Ranger School; the worst, if my memory serves me correctly, was a 25-mile march carrying 150lbs of equipment. Okay, maybe it was not that bad. So, let's say on the safe side it was only a 12-mile forced march carrying 75lbs worth of equipment. I did it. I made it. If you fail this march, you fail Ranger School and yes, get sent home.

Now, fast forward to my unit's 6 mile forced march with 50lbs. When I went into Ranger Mel mode, I had secret information. I already knew I could do 12 miles with at least 75lbs of equipment and not die, therefore I knew I had plenty of energy to spare to execute the 6-mile forced march with 50lbs. With that in mind, I made the informed decision I could focus on being the inspiring, enthusiastic, and optimistic leader my team needed. I knew I had a well of energy I could dip into when I put Ranger Mel into action. So, it was not really a case of "super human" Ranger Mel, just enthusiastic and optimistic Mel with information.

The same lessons have applied throughout my career. There is not a turnaround or transformation challenge that I believe I can't handle. The basis of that is I have been turning around and transforming businesses my entire career. There is not much that I have not seen in terms of issues within an organization: mission, vision, products, strategy, leadership, market place, marketing, operations, sales team, customer focus etc. I have seen, engaged, and won vs. almost every major challenge associated with a business in trouble. With that in mind, I believe I can face any business challenge and have a successful turnaround or transformation. So, it becomes easy for me to stay enthusiastic and optimistic in the face of dire business situations because I have done it before, Informed Enthusiasm and Optimism.

> *"Instead of worrying about what you cannot control, shift your energy to what you can create."*
> **Roy T Bennett**

Enthusiastic and Optimistic Leaders:

- Have courage and find ways to innovate and be creative, where others are fearful and seek safety and conservatism.

- See clear and stable paths forward, where others see cloudy skies and uncertainty.

- Believe every problem has a viable solution and that every obstacle can either be overcome or navigated around.

- Are inspiring communicators that elicit energetic enthusiasm. While I don't recommend you mirror my story by running up and down the office aisles shouting and encouraging people like a crazy person, I do recommend minimum power point slides and maximum interactive conversations with your team.

- Rally their teams with a vision of success and a better future. They paint a clear and executable picture of the success the team WILL achieve. They see the big picture and understand you only win when you get everyone across the finish line.

- Inspire extraordinary efforts from ordinary people. During that road march we talked about earlier, I can't put into words the emotions I felt when I watched soldiers grabbing, yelling, and encouraging their fellow soldiers to give their maximum effort to get to the finish line. There is no feeling that even comes close. Contagious optimism is a beautiful thing.

"Keep up your enthusiasm! There is nothing more contagious than exuberant enthusiasm."
Harry Houdini

For those who have seen me speak live, you know I am just a poor country boy from a farm in North Carolina. Despite that less than glamorous start in life, I have been blessed with a military and corporate career that I could have never dreamed of. I've also been fortunate enough to earn a reputation as a pretty good turnaround and transformational leader.

I earned this reputation over time from a humble start as the warehouse manager at PepsiCo in the little known small town of Moundsville, WV to the general manager of a multibillion dollar business at Dell to a stint as the North America President for Brinks, a billion-dollar financial service business with over 13,000 team members. In almost every case, there was a need for a business turnaround or transformation. The situation was dire, morale was low, and people were losing their jobs. While some engagements were tougher than others, I will bet a dollar and a cup of coffee that anyone who worked for me would say that, no matter how bad the situation, I was enthusiastic and optimistic.

My go-to response every time anyone asked me how I was doing was always an enthusiastic "Every Day is a GOOD DAY!" I believe that to the core of my being, and I have never let go of that eternal optimism. Every day we are alive is a GOOD DAY with new opportunities to grow, to be better than we were yesterday, and to take action to ensure we are better tomorrow.

"I'm an optimist. I've always believed the future is going to be better than the past. And I also believe I have a role in that. The great thing about human beings, myself in particular, is that I can change. I can do better. If you can get up every day, stay optimistic, and believe the future is better than the past, those few things get you through a lot of tough times."
Jeffrey Immelt

E&O leaders boost productivity, enhance employee morale, take care of customers, and have a positive impact on the bottom line. They have a way of convincing their teams they have the talent, energy, and stamina to achieve levels of performance far beyond what they thought possible.

"If you aren't fired with enthusiasm, you will be fired with enthusiasm."
Vince Lombardi

Ok Mel, I accept your view that enthusiasm and optimism are leadership force multipliers. Neither of those come naturally to me. What can I do? Here are a few suggestions that have worked for me during my toughest and most challenging times.

Celebrate Everything

Not just winning a big contract or hitting profit plan for the quarter. Celebrate a zero accident report for a location. Celebrate winning a small RFP at great margins. Celebrate your team members' birthdays and work anniversaries. Celebrate everything! It is a good habit, and it builds positive energy and momentum.

Avoid Negative Environments or Creating Negative Situations

While not always possible, this should always be your goal. Avoid pessimistic people and complainers at all costs. If they are in your organization, try to convert them. If you can't convert them, exit them. I don't care how talented they are; pessimism is dangerously contagious. Your organization will be healthier with them gone.

Focus on Strengths

Both yours and the people you lead. Strengths are more powerful and impactful than weaknesses, yet our human nature is to coach and judge ourselves and others by our weakness or shortcomings. Unlock the power of strengths. These will be positive conversations and create positive energy.

Focus on Positive Words, Tone and Body Language

Teach yourself to say yes more often than you say no. Say "yes, you can" more often than "no, you can't" especially in any written widely distributed correspondence. Negative words carry more impact when written.

Become aware of your tone and body language in meetings. Have a trusted advisor, usually a human resource leader, observe, evaluate, and give you feedback. Be receptive to that feedback. Speak with authority and confidence; sit up straight. No slouching! And try to avoid crossing your arms or your legs.

Positive Issue Management

Always ask people to bring you their challenges and issues, along with possible solutions to resolve. Assume every problem has a solution until the facts and tremendous effort prove otherwise.

Acceptance of the Uncontrollable

Manage or ignore the things you cannot change or control. Let go, to avoid uselessly dwelling on them.

Nurture a Culture of Optimism

Expect the team to Win! Expect any obstacle to be overcome. Even when you lose, focus on the opportunity to learn from the loss and win the next time.

Be Fit

Take care of yourself, physically, spiritually, and emotionally. You will feel better about yourself and the world around you. Your outlook will be more positive, and you will generate positive, optimistic energy.

Never Let Them See You Sweat

A calmness under pressure and stress always produces the aura and confidence of stability. When leaders are calm and positive under pressure, it has a proven performance enhancing effect on their teams. Some great movie examples immediately jump into my mind. Just because both examples involve Ranger leaders in combat is coincidental – NOT! You know me better than that by now!

First, in the movie Blackhawk Down, Tom Sizemore plays the character of Captain McKnight, and I am still moved and motivated by the scene where he is leading the convoy down the deadly Mogadishu Mile in his Humvee (HMMWV – High Mobility Multipurpose Wheeled Vehicle). He pulls up to the pinned down young soldiers with gunfire all around; you can see the bullets bouncing off the ground all around him. Faced with this chaos, he gets out, stands straight up like he is bulletproof with his hands on his hips, and yells for the soldiers frozen with fear to get up and get in the convoy vehicles so they could get to safety. They literally see his demeanor and make the decision based on their leader's calmness and confidence that it is ok for them to move, get up in the middle of the storm of bullets, and get into the vehicles. Even though it was obvious they needed to do this to save their lives, it took calmness, certainty, and the positive outlook of their leader to inspire them to action.

The second is the Tom Hanks character in Saving Private Ryan, Captain John Miller. In this scene, after taking his Rangers through storming the beaches in the gruesome and bloody landing at Normandy, he receives orders to get his team, go behind enemy lines, and attempt to find one solitary soldier, private Ryan. He shows only calmness, courage, and a positive attitude throughout the entire ordeal from getting his orders from his commander to briefing his team on their new mission to overcoming the ordeals and obstacles thrown at him as he goes to execute his mission. This courage and positive attitude inspired his team to accept, overcome the obstacles, and

186

accomplish the mission, another example of the heroic efforts a leader with calmness, courage and a positive attitude can get from their team members. That leads to my next best practice.

Fight the Fear

As a human, it is normal and healthy to have some measure of fear. As a leader, you must manage that fear so it does not infect your team members and their performance. There will be challenges and uncertainties, but there is an implicit expectation that these do not and will not cause fear in a leader. I don't believe there is any way you can be both optimistic about the future and fearful of that future. They cannot co-exist.

Energy Management

Optimism provides positive energy to any situation, and that energy builds more energy, creating a self-sustaining abundance of good energy. It has been my experience that being around a pessimistic or negative person literally drains energy from my body, mind, and spirit. You've probably experienced the same thing. How often do we accidentally avoid or even turn around and walk in the other direction to avoid an interaction with a person we know is negative or complains about everything? I've done it. If we are honest with ourselves, we all have probably done it. If you have never done it, and people seem to "accidentally" avoid you, then it's time to take stock. You may be the negative person everyone is steering clear of. Optimism is an energy producer for any leader.

"A pessimist sees the difficulty in every opportunity; an optimist sees the opportunity in every difficulty."
Winston S. Churchill.

I will end with some words from one of my personal heroes and one of the most optimistic leaders I have ever read about, Gen. Colin Powell. This is an excerpt from his 18 Lessons of Leadership.

Lesson 12 *"Perpetual optimism is a force multiplier."*

The ripple effect of a leader's enthusiasm and optimism is awesome. So is the impact of cynicism and pessimism. Leaders who whine and blame engender those same behaviors among their colleagues. I am not talking about stoically accepting organizational stupidity and performance incompetence with a "what, me worry?" smile. I am talking about a gung ho attitude that says, "we can change things here, we can achieve awesome goals, we can be the best." Spare me the grim litany of the "realist;" give me the unrealistic aspirations of the optimist any day."

RANGERS LEAD THE WAY!

Be Enthusiastic and Optimistic
Chapter Recap

- Leadership enthusiasm and optimism are a dynamic energy creating duo.
- Informed Optimism is a leadership force multiplier.
- Optimistic Leaders
    - Have courage and find ways to take risks to innovate and create.
    - Set clear and stable paths forward under adverse conditions.
    - Believe every problem has a viable solution.
    - Are inspiring communicators and rally their teams with a vision of success.
    - Inspire extraordinary efforts from ordinary people.
- Best practices for E&O Leadership
    - Celebrate everything.
    - Avoid negative environments or creating negative situations.
    - Focus on positive words, tone, and body language.
    - Accept the uncontrollable.
    - Never lose composure.
    - Fight fear with optimism.

Conclusion

The power of leadership and the impact of great leaders on people, organizations, and the world should not be underestimated. Almost every problem or crisis can be successfully navigated with great leadership. While we recognize the new normal for business chaos and that the business world has become more Volatile, Uncertain, Complex, and Ambiguous, we don't have to accept it as outside of our span of control. There are specific and dynamic actions leaders can take to make themselves and their organizations more V.U.C.A. prepared, savvy, and successful. The Parker Principles are designed to increase the impact and effect of leadership in the world of 21st Century business chaos.

Parker Principle #1: Leadership is Learning is the foundational and Cornerstone principle that **will** help you create a learning rationale, construct, and discipline that **will** enhance your ability to learn at the pace of business. It is a principle that **will** give you the tools to build and optimize your leadership savvy.

Parker Principle #2: Build Trust by Leading with Authenticity is a densely packed chapter, where we do a deep dive into the performance dividend of trusted leadership and the performance tax of distrust. There is a tremendous amount of information on how to recognize distrust within your organization and immediately executable techniques and best practices to build leadership and organizational trust. This is probably the single most important chapter in the book to read, reread, and assimilate. Without trust, a leader will be challenged to engage the other principles and maximize their leadership impact.

Parker Principle #3: Courageous Leadership- Dare to Dream and Dare to Fail is my all-time favorite Parker Principle because it goes into great detail on three of the most efficacious traits to Take The Limits Off leadership – Courage, Dreaming, and Failure. These characteristics are all about the power of heart – a brave heart, a visionary heart, and a heart of perseverance. When times are tough and challenging, this is the chapter to go back and reread for inspiration and resilience.

Parker Principle #4: Leadership is Relationships is the glue that holds together all Parker Principles. While we would like to believe otherwise, the world is powered by relationships. Whether in business or in personal life – relationships matter. This chapter provides significant depth on the power and criticality of relationships to great leadership. With techniques and best practices on communication, networking, mentorship, and sponsorship, this is a chapter I would review every six months to assess how well you are optimizing this principle. The building and maintenance of quality relationships is hard work and demands, attention, time, and energy. It is easy to "get lost" or distracted by the daily business chaos and not make the time for relationships. This chapter will help you withstand the chaos and navigate the path to great relationships.

As I am sure you noticed, the first four chapters were dense and information packed chapters. That is purposeful and by design. In my introduction, I refer to great leadership as magic. Magic has always been a combination of science and art. So is the magic of great leadership. These four chapters are focused on the science of leadership. There are many well-researched and proven techniques and best practices that, when executed, will have a measurable impact on your leadership. These chapters are filled with facts, figures, doctrine, and theory. They are grounded in the reasoning and logic of the mind.

The next six chapters focused more on the art of leadership, principles that every leader will absorb, internalize, and adopt in their own unique way. Leaders will view these principles through their own unique lens, colored by gender, race, religion, background, and prior life experiences. Principles like Listening, Responsibility, Humility, Belief, Confidence and Optimism have no 'right" answer. They only have your answer. These chapters will give you "tool savvy" for these force multipliers that will allow you to maximize innate strengths and minimize innate weaknesses. These chapters are less instructive and more educational, with real life stories on what these principles meant to me and how I turned them into leadership success.

By making the decision to read this book, you chose the path of learning, knowledge, and growth (personal and professional). That being said, you still have to put in the work. Everyone that graduates West Point or Ranger School is not guaranteed success. There are plenty of graduates from both that fail in their careers and life. I view each of these as defining teachable moments – opportunities to learn and grow. Each individual has to make the decision to learn and grow from these moments. That is no different from reading this book – it is a teachable moment, and only you can decide to turn this moment into the learning and growth that enables you to maximize your leadership impact.

I noted in my introduction that this book was a labor of love, but it was much more than that. Leadership is the labor that I love. Taking The Limits Off every leader is my mission and purpose. It is my hope that sharing my journey and the principles that governed it helps you take the limits off your leadership and that you see yourself in these pages and know you alone hold the power to your success. You alone can truly Take The Limits Off your career and your life.

RANGERS LEAD THE WAY!!!

The Parker Principles: 10 Leadership Force Multipliers

1. Leadership is Learning.
2. Build Trust by Leading with Authenticity.
3. Courageous Leadership: Dare to Dream and Dare to Fail!
4. Leadership is Relationships: Develop Real Relationships.
5. Be a Great Listener.
6. Own Your Power: No Excuses!
7. Embrace Humility.
8. Believe in Something.
9. Be Strong, Fit, and Confident.
10. Be Enthusiastic and Optimistic.

COMING SOON!!!

In a follow up to *THE PARKER PRINCIPLES: 10 Leadership Force Multipliers*, Mel is currently writing his next book, *Success Strategies for the Upwardly Mobile Executive*. *The Parker Principles* focused great leadership and maximizing the efficiency and effectiveness of your personal leadership. Great leaders also tend to be upwardly mobile executives. *Success Strategies* focuses specifically on what great leaders can do to accelerate their ascension up the corporate ladder to the C-Suite. These are specific, concise, and executable strategies guaranteed to accelerate any great leader's career.

- Develop a Living and Breathing Career Battle Plan
- Hyper focus on Customers
- Think for an Hour Every Day
- Keep a Journal
- Send a Handwritten Note Whenever Possible
- Get to Know Your People
- Know Your Numbers – Do Your Homework

Mel gives you a deep dive into the nuances, subtleties, and intricacies of each strategy. He also supplies tools, techniques, best practices, and real world examples of these strategies in action. Great leaders should have the opportunity to lead at the highest levels. This book will help you get there.

EXECUTIVE COACHING AND LEADERSHIP TRAINING

The main mission of The Parker Principles is to educate and inspire positive thoughtful reflection on your leadership style and potential. This aligns directly with the mission of Take The Limits Off, LLC to use these core leadership principles as the foundation to help unlock and maximize the leadership potential and effectiveness of senior leaders and executives. It is my position that, by learning and adopting great leadership principles, any leader can access their untapped potential and thereby maximize their contribution to the overall success of their teams and organization.

In today's Volatile, Uncertain, Complex, and Ambiguous world of business chaos, the quality of an organization's leaders is a competitive advantage and the best predictor of an organization's success. Board of Directors and Senior leaders everywhere demand this competitive advantage. There is also a recognition of the obstacles and challenges of leadership development. That leadership development must be purposeful, planned, and effective. Two of the most effective leadership development tools are leadership training and executive coaching. If you really want to raise the performance and results of your leaders and by default your organization, executive coaching and leadership training must be a mandatory and customized part of any leadership development strategy.

After having many senior executive roles in some of the best known global brands and organizations and as a business owner, I am totally convinced of the need for every successful organization to have a strong and vibrant leadership development strategy. Leadership has a dominate role in the success of the entire organization, so preparing potential leaders to lead and current leaders to excel is worth significant investment of time, energy, and resources.

At Take The Limits Off, we recognize all three of these items are scarce and under great ROI pressure. Our overriding belief is the more

196

efficient and effective the leader, the greater positive impact they have on the organization's ROI. We never take your investment for granted and hold ourselves accountable for delivering superior results. To learn more about how we can help augment your leadership development strategy, visit us at:

www.takethelimitsoff.com

to review the wide variety of keynotes, seminars, and workshops that can be customized to your company's needs and culture.

Let us help you Take The Limits Off your leadership and organizations potential.

-Mel Parker

ABOUT TAKE THE LIMITS OFF LLC

Take The Limits Off is a mission and purpose driven business consulting company focused on leadership optimization, business transformation, executive coaching, and talent management. We provide leaders and executives with the knowledge and environment to create trust-based, high performing teams and organizations. TTLO provides leaders with the tools and best practices to create engaged followers that deliver sustainable and predictable performance along with achieving desired results.

Our belief is that great leadership is the cornerstone and catalyst to an engaged workforce that takes ownership of their performance and results. We believe in a 360-degree engagement of leaders – their actions, behaviors, and how they think. This leader training and coaching concept is designed specifically to engage and unlock each leader's unique potential.

Mel provides keynotes, seminars, and workshops customized to the needs and culture of the organization. For detailed information or to sign up for The Parker Principles Leadership Newsletter and TTLO Blog, please visit www.takethelimitsoff.com. Some of Mel's most popular topics for keynotes, seminars, and workshops include:

- The Parker Principles: 10 Leadership Force Multipliers
- Success Strategies of the Upwardly Mobile Executive
- Executive Communication and Presence
- Transformation and Change Leadership
- Building and Leading High Performance Teams
- Value Creation – Leading a Culture of Innovation and Customer Focus
- Any one or combination of the 10 Leadership Force Multipliers

One Team One Dream

Leadership is a never-ending journey of knowledge and personal growth. Mel believes we all have something to teach and share. He would love you to share your insights, learnings, and experiences around leadership. Whether you just want to share privately with Mel or share widely with leaders everywhere, he would love to hear your stories. Please send comments and correspondence to: mystory@takethelimitsoff.com

CPSIA information can be obtained
at www.ICGtesting.com
Printed in the USA
FFHW02n1816310818
48189048-51918FF